A2

US Government and Politics

2nd Edition

Anthony J. Bennett

Philip Allan Updates, part of the Hodder Education Group, an Hachette Livre UK company, Market Place, Deddington, Oxfordshire OX15 0SE

Orders
Bookpoint Ltd, 130 Milton Park, Abingdon, Oxfordshire, OX14 4SB
tel: 01235 827720
fax: 01235 400454
e-mail: uk.orders@bookpoint.co.uk
Lines are open 9.00 a.m.–5.00 p.m., Monday to Saturday, with a 24-hour message answering service. You can also order through the Philip Allan Updates website: www.philipallan.co.uk

ISBN 978-0-86003-450-6

Cover illustration by John Spencer

Printed in Spain

Philip Allan Updates' policy is to use papers that are natural, renewable and recyclable products and made from wood grown in sustainable forests. The logging and manufacturing processes are expected to conform to the environmental regulations of the country of origin.

Contents

Introduction

'Those who fail to prepare, should prepare to fail.'
(Abraham Lincoln)

Using revision notes

This is not a textbook. You will doubtless have used one, and hopefully read a good deal of it, making detailed notes from it which you will now have to hand. It is worth stating that this is *not* a textbook, because it does *not* seek to tell you everything about and explain everything about US politics. You have been taught the course. You have participated in classes. You have read books and articles. You have written essays and exercises. These notes will *not* tell you how to write essays or answer the questions in the examination, but they *will* help you to do yourself justice, to better understand and learn the work you have already done and thus to be successful in the final examinations.

What these revision notes attempt to offer are:
- a concise guide to the main topics and issues
- up-to-date examples, facts and figures
- explanations of the points that might still confuse you
- a structure to help you revise
- some help with preparation for the exam itself

I have written them as if I were talking to the students in my classes, knowing what they find difficult to understand, knowing the mistakes that even the hard-working and well-prepared students can easily make. I have written them having marked literally thousands of essays on US politics, both from my own pupils and from those across the country as an A-level examiner. I trust what you read here will help you.

Eight of the nine topics covered in these revision notes deal with specific areas of American government and politics. The ninth looks at a number of key political concepts such as democracy, power and representation. It will be important at this level to have a good understanding of these important concepts. It will help you both to understand your American politics better and to make links with the UK government and politics you studied at AS.

Before you start

There are certain things you might need to do *before* you start using these notes. So, ask yourself the following questions:
(1) Have you made sure that the file in which you (hopefully) have kept all your work during this course is well organised? Are all the notes on each topic properly and clearly titled? Are they grouped together under topic headings? (Coloured file dividers are very useful for this.) Have you recently refreshed your memory as to exactly what you've got in the file?
(2) Have you seen copies of past (or example) papers? Do you know the kind of questions you are going to have to answer? Have you grouped questions together under your revision topic headings? (This will help you spot the focus of questions on particular topics.)

(3) Have you subscribed to any journals (such as *Politics Review*) during this course? If you have, have you noted (or highlighted) them, and do you have them in your file? (This will probably mean 'cannibalising' the magazine.)

(4) Have you worked out a revision plan? This means dividing up the course into bite-size pieces, deciding when each is going to be revised so that the revision process is completed well in advance of the examination itself?

If the answer to all these questions is 'yes', keep reading. If not, do it!

How to revise

Students are often told to 'revise'. But do you actually know what that entails? Revision involves a number of tasks:

- **Re-familiarising** yourself with work completed some time ago.
- **Organising** your material into manageable pieces.
- **Learning** the work.

It all takes time so start early, especially on the first two of these tasks. This will help with the third when it becomes time to do that as well.

Once the examination time approaches, you will probably find that classes will finish and you are on your own, often with whole days having to be set aside for revision. Days that you are setting aside for your own revision can be divided into three three-hour sessions: morning, afternoon, evening. Aim to work for two of them each day. Start early. End early. Get to bed early. You wouldn't be amused if you were asked to sit an exam at midnight. Don't do your revision then either! If you are organised, disciplined and start early enough, it shouldn't be necessary.

For each of these work sessions, set yourself realistic tasks to complete in the allotted time. And stick to them. Revision is not just shutting yourself away in a room with a book open in front of you. And as much as possible, write things down. It helps concentration.

Talking of concentration, get those obvious distractions well out of sight and reach: the computer games, the phone (mobile or otherwise), the television, the (non-academic!) magazines. If someone disturbs you, tell them (politely) to go away. Decide when — and for how long — you are going to allow yourself a break. (A 10-minute break every hour would not be unreasonable.)

When it comes to committing information to memory, how do you know that you have actually learnt it? The danger here is to mistake what I call 'instant recall' for 'memorising' something. Most of us can instantly repeat something we've just been told. But that does not mean that we have memorised it. (Ever tried remembering someone's phone number the day after they verbally told you what it was?) The recipe for success is to test yourself, first after a few hours, then after a number of hours, then after a day, then after a few days. You will soon see what you can and can't recall. This is why it is so important not to leave this task too late. The parallel I often cite to my students is of the person who goes into the supermarket 5 minutes before closing-time on Christmas Eve to do the entire family shopping. There just isn't time and Christmas lunch is likely to be a fairly disappointing affair in that household. Similarly, your examination results will be 'a fairly disappointing affair' if you don't start early enough and give yourself sufficient time.

What to revise

Over the years, some (unwise) students have sometimes told me after the examination: '*My* questions didn't come up.' I often wondered what they meant. Did they not realise that the exam paper was being set by someone else? Did they imagine they could write the questions as well as the answers? Sadly, of course, only *the examiner's* questions ever come up in an exam! I knew what they meant, of course: 'The (few) topics I revised were not asked.' Tough! They probably didn't learn enough topics. Don't play Russian roulette with your exam chances.

Not only do you need to revise plenty of topics, but you also need to learn more than just facts, as important as they are. Most candidates are going to know the facts. What examiners will be looking for are **up-to-date examples**. So many A-level answers I have marked have contained either no examples at all or ones that were needlessly dated. I didn't, for example, want to see references to the Kennedy/Nixon election of 1960 when the point could just as well be illustrated from the Bush/Gore election of 2000. The other feature that will make your answer stand out will be to include some scholarly quotations to back up your argument. This could be something from a noted author on the subject. Even in these revision notes, you will find a few such quotations from people like Richard Neustadt, Richard Fenno and Anthony King. Or it could be a quotation from an article you read in *Politics Review*. Quotations don't need to be long. This is not English literature! Something short and punchy is excellent. So look out for quotations to learn on major topics.

Remember, the recipe for good essays at this level is **logical argument backed up by relevant examples**.

The day of the examination

Here there are a number of rules of thumb:

(1) Arrive in good time — not too early, but certainly not at the last minute.

(2) Have with you everything you need which, for US politics, is likely to mean two pens (black roller-balls are the best) plus anything you need (and are allowed) in the way of bottled water, sweets, cuddly toys or mascots.

(3) Once in the exam room, remind yourself of the length of the exam and the number of questions you have to answer, working out the length of time you can afford on each question (as soon as you can, write down the times when you should be starting your second, third, fourth questions etc.)

(4) Once you are told you may begin, **read every question carefully**.

(5) Quickly rule out those you cannot attempt and decide which to do amongst those you can.

(6) Plan your answers, deciding the main points you need to make and the order in which you are going to make them.

(7) Keep an eye on the time.

(8) *Never* leave the examination room before the end of the allotted time, even if the rules at your Centre allow you to do so.

There is always the temptation for the well-prepared candidate to disadvantage themselves by writing material that is not asked for by the question. It's a kind of 'I know it, so I'm going tell you' mentality. I remember marking an A-level essay which was some nine sides(!) in length. The candidate had been asked the question: 'Why has the US Constitution been subjected to so few amendments?' The main focus I was looking for was the three reasons: the foresight of the founding fathers in writing an adaptable document; the difficulty of the amendment process; and the Supreme Court's ability to make 'interpretative amendments' through its power of judicial review. But this candidate spent pages telling me all about the Philadelphia Convention, the Founding Fathers (complete with biographies on some!), as well as detailing the content of virtually all the Articles and Amendments of the Constitution. It was so frustrating. They clearly knew their stuff. They had clearly been well taught and prepared very thoroughly. But it just was *not relevant*.

I sometimes use the analogy that revising for examinations is rather like packing your suitcase to go on a summer holiday. Some people don't pack enough and when the weather turns warm and sunny, they don't have the swimwear or the beach towel that they now wish they had packed. Silly. But others pack everything from raincoat, hat and scarf to swimwear and beach towel. The weather is fine and sunny. But it would be such a shame not to wear the raincoat, hat and scarf having brought them. So while everyone else is strolling along the beach in swimwear, they are sporting the rainwear! Equally silly. Sensible folk will pack more than they need, but not use it. **Sensible candidates will learn more than they need, but not use it**.

Your teacher will doubtless have told you to **'answer the question'**. It sounds so obvious — but it isn't. To ensure that you do this, adopt the following strategy. Before attempting to answer a question ask yourself:
- Is there anything in the question that requires definition, clarification or explanation?
- What is the key word or phrase of the question?

You will often need to begin your answer by defining, clarifying or explaining things. For example, imagine you are responding to the question: 'Examine the claim that the process for selecting presidential candidates is undemocratic.' Well, what is 'the process for selecting presidential candidates?' You will need to explain. And what does the word 'undemocratic' mean? You will need to clarify. Only then can you answer the question.

Whatever you identify as the 'key word or phrase' of the question should be used as the focus for your answer. So in the example just given, the key word is 'undemocratic'. The best answers will be organised along the following lines:
(1) An explanation of 'the process for selecting presidential candidates'.
(2) A definition/clarification of the term 'undemocratic'.
(3) Arguments to support the claim.
(4) Arguments against the claim.

There is absolutely no doubt that an essay written according to this plan will answer the question.

Revision notes structure

These notes have been structured into nine topics as follows:
- Topic 1   The Constitution
- Topic 2   Presidential elections
- Topic 3   Political parties
- Topic 4   Pressure groups
- Topic 5   Congress

- Topic 6   The presidency
- Topic 7   The vice-presidency
- Topic 8   The Supreme Court
- Topic 9   Key political concepts

These topics are then further divided as follows:

• Main headings	**A**	**B**	**C**
• Subdivisions	*1*	*2*	*3*
• Subdivided again	**1.1**	**1.2**	**1.3**
• Subdivided yet again	**1.1a**	**1.1b**	**1.1c**

Each page is split into two columns. On the right you will find the main body of the text and tables. On the left you will find 'comments' that should help you understand the text and avoid common errors and misunderstandings.

Acknowledgements

I wish to acknowledge all the help and advice given by the staff at Philip Allan Updates and, most particularly, by David Cross. Furthermore, I owe a considerable debt to my pupils at Charterhouse over many years, not only for their unfailing enthusiasm but also for their patience as I have 'tried out' my ideas on them. I'm afraid they will recognise too many of the quips and admonitions contained in these pages. But whilst the credit is shared, the blame for any errors which remain is mine alone. 'The buck stops here!' Good luck!

Anthony J. Bennett

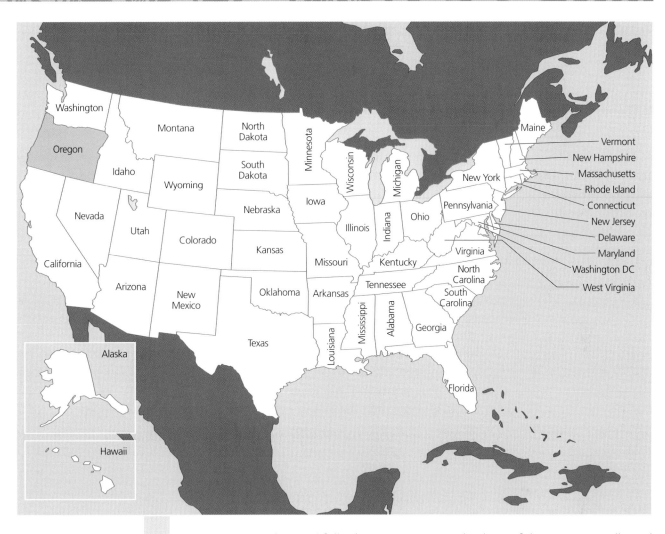

Shaded in the map above.

In order to understand fully the government and politics of the USA, you will need to have some comprehension of how the nation was formed and how the Constitution came to be written in 1787. You will also need to understand the basic principles that underlie the Constitution — **separation of powers**, **checks and balances**, and **federalism**. Remember that the USA is a vast country. You can fit the entire UK into Oregon. Even the 48 contiguous states — not counting Alaska and Hawaii — encompass over 3,000 miles (4,800 kilometres) and four time zones. It's as far from New York to Los Angeles as it is from New York to London. When it's midday in London and 7 a.m. in New York, it's still only 4 a.m. in California. **Vastness** is one characteristic of America. **Diversity** is another, diversity in terms of race, culture, language, religion, climate and economy. The USA needs a particular kind of governmental and political structure to cope with all this.

The topic is divided into the following five major headings:

A Before the Constitution
B The Constitution
C Separation of powers
D Checks and balances
E Federalism

A Before the Constitution

1 *1776–83*

You don't need to know the details of American history for this course in government and politics. But it helps to have a working knowledge of what came before the founding of the USA. The order in which things happened is more important than the dates themselves.

Here is a very brief survey of what occurred in the years before the writing of the American Constitution:

- **1776:** the 13 colonies on the eastern seaboard of North America declared their independence from Great Britain in the **Declaration of Independence**.
- **1776–83:** there followed the **War of Independence** between the former colonies and Great Britain.
- **1781:** the newly independent colonies decided to establish a **confederacy** — a loose association of states in which almost all political power rests with the individual states — by the **Articles of Confederation**.

Between 1781 and 1787 there was almost no national government. Virtually all power resided with the states. Virginians ruled Virginia. New Yorkers ruled New York, and so on. That was what they had fought to gain from Britain. There was no president. There was no national court. There was a Congress, but it could not pass any laws; it was merely a debating chamber. The states squabbled amongst each other, principally over trade (taxes charged by each state for goods to pass through) and money (each state had its own currency). Chaos ensued.

To help bring order out of chaos, the **Philadelphia Convention** convened in the summer of 1787.

2 *The Philadelphia Convention*

Rhode Island delegates were fearful that the hard-won gains of the War of Independence would be lost and refused to attend.

At this time, Virginia was the state with the largest population.

Again, all you need to know here are the basic facts:
- It was convened in Philadelphia on 25 May 1787.
- Delegates from the 13 states were invited.
- 55 of the invited 74 turned up — Rhode Island was the only state to send no delegates.
- It was presided over by **George Washington**.
- Also present were James Madison, Thomas Jefferson and Alexander Hamilton.
- Although the stated purpose of the Convention was merely to **revise** the Articles of Confederation, they decided to scrap them and write a new Constitution.
- Divisions arose between the small-population and large-population states.
- The **Virginia Plan** set out the wishes of the large-population states.
- The **New Jersey Plan** set out those of the small-population states.
- The **Connecticut Compromise** (often called 'the Great Compromise') provided the basis for agreement.
- The new Constitution was written by these 55 delegates who became known as the **Founding Fathers**.

B The Constitution

1 Introduction

This is where your knowledge and understanding need to become much more detailed.

This is the kind of 'scholarly quotation' you ought to try and get into an essay. Short but insightful.

The Founding Fathers decided to write a new Constitution. This involved making a whole number of **compromises**. Indeed, 'compromise' is a key word to aid full understanding of American government and politics. The Constitution is made up of a whole series of compromises, and to govern — whether you are the president or a member of Congress — involves making compromises. That is what the Founding Fathers wanted. Alistair Cooke has written that the American Constitution was founded upon three great principles: 'compromise, compromise and compromise'.

Here are three of the major compromises embodied in the new Constitution.

2 The three compromises

2.1 The form of government

Notice 'equally important' — not just trivial matters such as keeping the roads clean.

Under Great Britain, the colonies had been ruled under a **unitary** form of government. All political power rested with Great Britain, none with the colonies themselves. The colonists disliked this. As we have just seen, from 1781 they had been ruled by a **confederal** form of government where virtually all political power rested with the individual states, very little with the national government. This had simply not worked. The compromise was to devise a new form of government — a **federal** form of government. This gives some political power to the national (or federal) government but other, equally important, powers to the state governments.

2.2 The representation of the states

'Bicameral' is the technical phrase — made up of two houses or 'chambers'.

Don't use the phrase 'proportional representation'. It isn't.

In the new Congress, the large-population states wanted representation to be proportional to population. The bigger the population of a state, the more representatives it would have in the new Congress. The small-population states wanted equal representation. The compromise was to have a Congress made up of two houses — the House of Representatives and the Senate. In the House of Representatives, there would be representation proportional to population. In the Senate, there would be equal representation for all states, regardless of population.

2.3 The choosing of the president

'Electors' with a capital 'E' to avoid misunderstanding.

There were many different suggestions about how to choose the president. Some thought the president should be **appointed**. Others thought the president should be **directly elected** by the people. The compromise was to have the president **indirectly elected** by an Electoral College (see Topic 2.5.2). The people would elect the Electoral College and the 'Electors' within the Electoral College would choose the president.

3   The Constitution in outline

You should be familiar with the first three Articles of the Constitution:

- Article I: established that **the Congress** was to be made up of two chambers; laid down methods of election, terms of office and powers (see Topic 5).
- Article II: established **a President of the USA**; laid down methods of election, terms of office and powers (see Topic 6).
- Article III: established the **United States Supreme Court**; laid down the judges' terms of office and their jurisdiction (see Topic 8).

Attached to the first seven Articles were ten Amendments known as **the Bill of Rights**. You should be familiar with Amendments I, II, V, VIII and X.

4   Amending the Constitution

Amending the Constitution is a two-stage process: **proposal** and **ratification** (see Table 1.1).

(1) Proposals to amend the Constitution can be made either by Congress with **a two-thirds majority** in favour in **both houses**, or by a national Constitutional Convention called at the request of two-thirds of the state legislatures. The latter has never been used.

(2) Ratification can be made either by **three-quarters of the state legislatures** or by three-quarters of the states holding a Constitutional Convention. The latter has been used only once — to ratify the 21st Amendment in 1933.

Note that this three-quarters figure concerns the proportion of states that must ratify, not the majority by which they must ratify the Amendment.

Amendments proposed by:	Amendments ratified by:
Either **Congress:** two-thirds majority in both houses required or **National Constitutional Convention:** called by at least two-thirds of the states (never used)	Either **State legislatures:** three-quarters of the state legislatures must vote to ratify often within a stated time limit or **State Constitutional Conventions:** three-quarters of the states must hold Conventions and vote to ratify

Table 1.1 Procedures for amending the Constitution

Following the ratification of the Bill of Rights in 1791, there have been 17 further amendments in 210 years. Two of these 17 cancel each other out: the 18th and 21st Amendments imposing and then ending the prohibition of alcohol.

Numerous amendments have been proposed but not ratified. Recent examples include proposals to:

- guarantee equal rights for women
- require the federal government to pass a balanced budget
- impose term limits on members of Congress
- forbid desecration of the American flag

As Table 1.2 shows, in the 6-year period between 1995 and 2000, Congress voted 17 times on constitutional amendments — 12 times in the House, 5 times in the Senate. The House passed amendments on four occasions, three being on the

same amendment — to forbid flag desecration. But the Senate rejected every amendment it considered during this time, including the Balanced Budget Amendment in three successive years.

In the final column of Table 1.2, 'passed' means 'passed in this house by a two-thirds majority'; 'rejected' means 'failed in this house to gain a two-thirds majority'.

Date	Chamber	Subject	Vote	Passed/Rejected
1995				
28 January	House	Balanced budget	300–132	Passed
2 March	Senate	Balanced budget	65–35	Rejected
29 March	House	Term limits	227–204	Rejected
28 June	House	Flag desecration	312–120	Passed
12 December	Senate	Flag desecration	62–36	Rejected
1996				
15 April	House	Tax limitation	243–177	Rejected
6 June	Senate	Balanced budget	64–35	Rejected
1997				
12 February	House	Term limits	217–211	Rejected
4 March	Senate	Balanced budget	66–34	Rejected
15 April	House	Tax limitation	233–190	Rejected
12 June	House	Flag desecration	310–114	Passed
1998				
22 April	House	Tax limitation	238–186	Rejected
4 June	House	School prayers	224–203	Rejected
1999				
15 April	House	Tax limitation	229–199	Rejected
24 June	House	Flag desecration	305–124	Passed
2000				
29 March	Senate	Flag desecration	63–37	Rejected
12 April	House	Tax limitation	234–192	Rejected

Table 1.2 Attempts to initiate constitutional amendments in Congress, 1995–2000

C Separation of powers

1 Definition

Watch for spelling of 'sep**a**ration'.'Legisla*ture*' is the noun; 'legisla*tive*' is the adjective. Don't confuse the two. It is 'the legislature' or 'the legislative branch'.

The separation of powers is a theory of government by which power is divided between three branches of government — the legislature, the executive and the judiciary — each acting both independently and interdependently.

2 Explanation

The functions of government can be divided into three:

(1) Legislating: this is done by the **legislature** which **makes the laws**.

'Executing' means 'carrying out'.

(2) Executing: this is done by the **executive** which **carries out the laws**.

(3) Enforcing: this is done by the **judiciary**, which **enforces the laws**. The judiciary also **interprets the laws**, and in the USA, where there is a written Constitution, **interprets the Constitution** (the 'supreme law').

The legislature	Makes the laws	Congress
The executive	Carries out the laws	The president and the federal bureaucracy
The judiciary	Enforces and interprets the laws	The Supreme Court and the Appeal and Trial Courts

Table 1.3 The three branches of government

This is a most important paragraph. Make sure you understand it fully.

Another of those 'scholarly quotations' for your essays.

But the functions are not completely separated. Indeed, the term 'separation of powers' is rather confusing. For it is not the 'powers' that are separate but the institutions. As Richard Neustadt has stated: 'The Constitutional Convention of 1787 is supposed to have created a government of "separated powers". It did nothing of the sort. Rather, it created a government of **separated institutions sharing powers**.' So the theory is more accurately described as a theory of **'shared powers'** than 'separated powers'. The institutions — the Congress, the presidency and the courts — are indeed separate. But their powers are shared. This sharing of powers is what is called **'checks and balances'**.

D Checks and balances

1 Definition

Checks and balances is a theory of government by which each of the three branches of government — the legislature, the executive and the judiciary — exercise checks upon the powers and actions of the others.

2 Explanation

Professor S. E. Finer likened the president and Congress to 'two halves of a bank note, each useless without the other'.

Think of the government's three branches of government as a bank note cut into three pieces. Each is useless without the other. But together they are useful. On their own, the Congress, the president and the Supreme Court can do little or nothing. To get things done, they must **cooperate**. That is what the Founding Fathers wanted, to avoid too much power being vested in one branch. It would thus avoid what they most feared, which was tyranny. The Founding Fathers were especially worried about the president becoming something of a tyrant, so they subjected the executive branch to the most comprehensive set of checks. Also keep in mind that the checks and balances between the legislature and the executive (the Congress and the president) can become even more complicated when these two branches are controlled by different political parties. In the period from January 1969 to January 2001, for only 6 of the 32 years did the same party control both branches of government. This can lead to **gridlock**, a term derived from traffic jams in American cities where the intersections of their grid-patterned streets become jammed and as a result nothing can move.

3 Examples

These are laid out in Table 1.4.

Checks on → / Checks by ↓	The legislature	The executive	The judiciary
The legislature		• Amend/delay/reject the president's legislation • Override the president's veto • Control of the budget • Senate's power to confirm numerous appointments made by the president • Senate's power to ratify treaties negotiated by the president • Declare war • Investigation • Impeachment, trial, conviction and removal from office of any member of the executive branch, including the president	• Senate's power to confirm appointments made by the president • Initiate constitutional amendments • Impeachment, trial, conviction and removal from office of any member of the judiciary
The executive	• Recommend legislation • Veto legislation • Call Congress into special session		• Appointment of judges • Pardon
The judiciary	• Judicial review: the power to declare Acts of Congress unconstitutional	• Judicial review: the power to declare actions of any member of the executive branch — including the president — unconstitutional	

Table 1.4 Checks and balances

E Federalism

1 Definition

Federalism is a theory of government by which power is divided between a national government and state governments, each having their own areas of substantive jurisdiction.

'Substantive jurisdiction' = important powers.

2 Explanation

Federalism involves a certain level of **decentralisation**. As already explained, it is a compromise between a highly centralised form of government on the one hand and a loose confederation of independent states on the other. In other words, it is a compromise between the two experiences America had before 1787

— government by Great Britain, and government by the Articles of Confederation. It is a very appropriate form of government for a country as large and diverse as the USA. It allows for both national unity as well as regional and local diversity.

3 *Federalism and the Constitution*

Nowhere are the words 'federal' or 'federalism' to be found in the American Constitution. How, then, is it written into this document?

- By Articles I, II and III, which lay out the powers of the national government.
- By Amendment X, which guarantees that all the remaining powers 'are reserved to the states and to the people'.

It is important to remember the political atmosphere in which the Constitution was drawn up. The former British colonies had successfully got rid of what they saw as the distant, autocratic and highly centralised government of Great Britain. They had then tried to allow each of the individual states to govern themselves, but this had resulted in chaos. So the new Constitution had somehow to square the circle. It had to 'form a more perfect Union' — that is, provide some central authority — and also to protect the interests of the individual states. So the Constitution had to do a number of potentially conflicting things at once:

- It had to give certain **exclusive powers** to the new national (federal) government. So only the national government could coin money, negotiate treaties, tax imports and exports or maintain troops in peacetime.
- It had to offer guarantees of **states' rights**. So, for example, the states were guaranteed equal representation in the Senate, that their borders would not be changed without their consent and that the Constitution could not be amended without the agreement of three-quarters of them.
- It had to make clear that there were also **states' responsibilities**. Each state had to recognise the laws of each other state by, for example, returning fugitives.

All this the Constitution did. But what it failed to do — and wisely so — was to lay down any definite line between the **concurrent powers** of the national and state governments. This has meant that the concept of federalism has been able to develop over the subsequent two centuries. Although, for example, in Article I Congress was given specific powers to 'coin money', 'declare war' and 'raise and support armies', it was also given the power 'to provide for the common defense and general welfare of the United States'. And it was also given the power to 'make all laws which shall be necessary and proper for carrying into execution the foregoing powers'. This latter clause of Article I is known as the **elastic clause** of the Constitution, as it has allowed the powers of the national government to be stretched a good deal since 1787.

4 *The development of federalism*

Federalism is not a fixed concept. It is ever changing. As America has changed, so has the concept of federalism.

An extract from the opening sentence of the Preamble to the Constitution: 'We the people, in order to form…'.

The most significant changes that have occurred in the USA since 1787 and have led to the development and evolution of federalism are:

- westward expansion
- the growth in population
- industrialisation
- improvements in communication — by road, rail and air, as well as by post, telephone, radio, television, fax and e-mail
- America's foreign policy role and world-power status

During the latter part of the nineteenth century and the first two-thirds of the twentieth century, all these five factors led to an increased role for the federal government and a decline in the power of state governments. But during the final third of the twentieth century, there was a distinct move in the opposite direction as Americans wanted to see more power and more decisions devolved to the states wherever this was possible. It is therefore possible to discern three distinct phases of federalism in America:

(1) Dual federalism (1780s–1920s) — an era in which the state governments had significant power.

(2) Cooperative federalism (1930s–1960s) — an era in which the federal government became more and more powerful, sometimes at the expense of the states. This is associated with the Democratic presidents Franklin Roosevelt ('The New Deal'), Truman ('The Fair Deal'), Kennedy ('The New Frontier') and Johnson ('The Great Society'), as well as the USA becoming a world power. The federal government administered **categorical grants**, schemes by which Washington was able to stipulate how federal tax dollars were used by the states.

(3) New federalism (1970s–present) — an era in which, wherever possible, power was devolved to the states. This is associated with the Republican presidents Nixon, Ford, Reagan and George Bush, but was also partly adopted by Clinton in the 1990s. The federal government gradually moved towards **block grants** and **revenue-sharing** by which Washington allowed the states greater independence in how federal tax dollars were spent.

As a result of policies pursued by administrations of both parties — though especially Republicans — over the last 30 years, the states have seen quite a significant increase in their autonomy and power. Decentralisation and states' rights are once again the buzz words in American politics. This has come about through a number of important developments:

- The reduction of federal government economic aid to the states.
- A perception that the federal government programmes such as FDR's New Deal and Johnson's Great Society had not been as successful as at first thought.
- A belief that the federal government had simply failed to tackle some pressing social problems such as those associated with gun crime, drugs, abortion, welfare and poverty.
- This led to a widespread distrust and scepticism of the federal government and 'Washington politicians'.
- Decisions by the mainly Republican-appointed Supreme Court, which began to limit the scope of the federal government in such cases as *United States v. Lopez* (1995) and *Printz v. United States* (1997) while upholding states' rights in such

Dates are deliberately vague. Avoid being too precise. These were gradual changes.

President Clinton famously remarked (1996): 'The era of big government is over.'

cases as *Webster v. Reproductive Health Services* (1989) and *Planned Parenthood of Southeastern Pennsylvania v. Casey* (1992) (see Topic 8.C for details).

- The Republican domination of the White House during the 1970s and 1980s and of Congress after 1994, which allowed conservative politicians to push their states' rights agenda.
- The election of a significant number of Republican state governors during the 1990s, which led to state-based innovations in such states as New Jersey (under Governor Christine Todd Whitman) and Wisconsin (under Governor Tommy Thompson).

5   *The consequences of federalism*

You should be aware of the way in which federalism affects so many aspects of US government and politics. Here are a few important ways:

- Tremendous variation in state laws concerning such matters as the age at which one can marry, drive a car and must attend school.
- Variation in penalties for law-breaking from state to state.
- Complexity of the American legal system, having both national and state courts.
- Each state not only has its own laws and courts but its own Constitution.
- Complexity of the tax system: income tax (federal and state); state property taxes; local sales taxes.
- All elections in the USA are state-based, run largely under state law.
- The frequency and number of elections.
- Political parties are decentralised and largely state-based.
- Regional diversity (the South, the Midwest, the Northeast etc.) and regional considerations when making appointments to, for example, the cabinet, or when 'balancing the ticket' in the presidential election.

See Topic 2.

See Topic 3.

See Topic 6.

Article	Content	Ratified
I	The powers etc. of the legislature	1787
II	The powers etc. of the executive	1787
III	The powers etc. of the judiciary	1787
IV	Federal–state and state–state relationships	1787
V	Amendment procedures	1787
VI	Miscellaneous	1787
VII	Ratification procedure for the Constitution	1787

Amendment	Content	Ratified
I	Freedom of religion, press, speech, assembly	1791
II	Right to bear arms	1791
III	Privacy of property owners	1791
IV	Freedom from unreasonable searches and seizures	1791
V	Rights of accused persons; due process clause	1791
VI	Rights when on trial	1791
VII	Common-law suits	1791
VIII	Prohibition of excessive bail and 'cruel and unusual' punishments	1791
IX	Reserved rights to the people	1791
X	Reserved rights to the states	1791
XI	Limits of judicial power	1795
XII	Revision of Electoral College procedure	1804
XIII	Prohibition of slavery	1865
XIV	Guarantee of 'equal protection' for all; 'due process' clause applied to the states	1868
XV	Blacks given voting rights	1870
XVI	Congress given power to tax incomes	1913
XVII	Direct election of Senators	1913
[XVIII]	[Prohibition of alcohol]	1919
XIX	Women given voting rights	1920
XX	Presidential and congressional terms to begin in January	1933
XXI	Repealed 18th Amendment	1933
XXII	Two-term limit for the president	1951
XXIII	Washington DC given voting rights in presidential elections	1961
XXIV	Poll tax prohibited as requirement for voting	1964
XXV	Presidential disability and succession	1967
XXVI	Voting age lowered to 18	1971
XXVII	Limits on timing of congressional pay rises	1992

Table 1.5 The Constitution in brief

Even the UK media cover quite a bit about US presidential elections. But that does not necessarily mean that we — or they — fully understand what is going on. There are numerous things over which confusion readily occurs. From a glance at the media coverage on this side of the Atlantic, it would be tempting to think that there were no other elections in the USA. Far from it. There are elections for both houses of Congress as well as elections at state and local level for governors, state legislators, city mayors and a host of other elected officials. But in this topic, we are concerned only with presidential elections. We shall try to establish what happens, why people vote as they do, and the role that the media and money play in the whole electoral process in the USA.

Year	Candidates	Popular vote (%)	Electoral College vote
1964	**Lyndon Johnson/Hubert Humphrey (D)**	61.0	486
	Barry Goldwater/William Miller (R)	38.5	52
1968	**Richard Nixon/Spiro Agnew (R)**	43.2	301
	Hubert Humphrey/Edmund Muskie (D)	42.7	191
	George Wallace/Curtis LeMay (I)	13.5	46
1972	**Richard Nixon/Spiro Agnew (R)**	60.7	520
	George McGovern/Sargent Shriver (D)	37.5	17
1976	**Jimmy Carter/Walter Mondale (D)**	50.1	297
	Gerald Ford/Bob Dole (R)	48.0	240
1980	**Ronald Reagan/George Bush (R)**	50.7	489
	Jimmy Carter/Walter Mondale (D)	41.0	49
1984	**Ronald Reagan/George Bush (R)**	58.8	525
	Walter Mondale/Geraldine Ferraro (D)	40.6	13
1988	**George Bush/Dan Quayle (R)**	53.4	426
	Michael Dukakis/Lloyd Bentsen (D)	45.6	111
1992	**Bill Clinton/Al Gore (D)**	43.0	370
	George Bush/Dan Quayle (R)	37.5	168
	Ross Perot/James Stockdale (I)	18.9	0
1996	**Bill Clinton/Al Gore (D)**	49.2	379
	Bob Dole/Jack Kemp (R)	40.7	159
2000	**George W. Bush/Dick Cheney (R)**	47.9	271
	Al Gore/Joe Lieberman (D)	48.4	266
2004	**George W. Bush/Dick Cheney (R)**	50.7	286
	John Kerry/John Edwards (D)	48.3	252

Table 2.1 Presidential election results, 1964–2004 (winners in bold)

The topic is divided into the following four major headings:

A The election process
B Voting behaviour
C Money
D The media

A The election process

1 An overview

Presidential elections occur:

- every 4 years
- in years divisible by four: 1992, 1996, 2000, 2004 etc.
- on the Tuesday after the first Monday in November (i.e. between 2 November and 8 November)

The Constitution (Article II) states that to be eligible to be president a person must:

- be a natural-born US citizen
- be at least 35 years of age
- have been resident in the USA for at least 14 years

The Constitution (Amendment XXII, passed in 1951) also states that a person cannot serve more than two terms as president.

A presidential election can be thought of as occurring in **four** stages. The first two are concerned with **choosing the candidates**; the second two are concerned with **electing the president.**

Stage	Functions	Occurs
1. Primaries and caucuses	(i) Show popularity of candidates (ii) Choose delegates to attend the National Party Conventions	Late January–early June
2. National Party Conventions	(i) Choose presidential candidate (ii) Choose vice-presidential candidate (iii) Decide on party platform	July–August (each lasts 4 days)
3. General election campaign	The campaign between candidates of the various parties	September, October, first week of November
4. Election day and Electoral College votes	Elect the president and vice-president through the Electoral College	Election day: Tuesday after the first Monday in November Electoral College votes: Monday after the second Wednesday in December

Table 2.2 Presidential elections: a four-stage process

2 Primaries

2.1 Definitions

A presidential primary is an election to select a party's candidate for the presidency. Some states with a small population spread over a large geographic area often hold **caucuses** instead of a primary. The states that held caucuses rather than a primary in 2004 included Iowa, Hawaii, North Dakota, Minnesota and Nevada.

So if 1 November is a Tuesday, the presidential election is on 8 November.

In other words, born as a US citizen.

This is why Bill Clinton could not be a candidate for president in 2000 and can never be again.

In exam questions do be careful to see the difference between the phrases 'selecting presidential candidates' and 'electing the president'.

A caucus is a series of meetings to select a party's candidate for the presidency.

2.2 Functions

Presidential primaries have two main functions:

(1) To show the popularity of presidential candidates; primaries can therefore be thought of as political 'beauty contests'.

(2) To choose delegates to go to the National Party Conventions.

2.3 How primaries are run

Presidential primaries are run under **state** law, not federal law. That means there are potentially 50 different ways of running primaries, which is very confusing. Just keep to the main rules of thumb. You need to know that states decide **six** important things about primaries:

(1) Whether to hold a primary or a caucus. The vast majority of states now hold primaries.

(2) When to hold the primary. Primaries tend to be held between late January and early June. But each state will decide exactly when within that 4–5-month period to schedule their primary: whether to go early or late, to go for a date on their own or to coincide it with other, maybe neighbouring, states.

(3) How to conduct the primary. Recently, some states have experimented with postal voting and even electronic voting via the Internet.

(4) Who exactly can vote in the primary. It is important to understand that any registered voter can vote in a primary in any state. But in some states, when you register you are asked to declare your party affiliation — whether you consider yourself to be a Democrat or Republican. Some states then allow only registered Democrats to vote in the Democratic primary and only registered Republicans to vote in the Republican primary. This is known as a **closed primary**. Other states don't bother with establishing party affiliation. They allow any registered voter to decide, on the day of the primary, whether they want to vote in the Democratic primary or the Republican primary. This is known as an **open primary**.

(5) Who can be on the ballot. States have their own laws about who gets on the ballot. In some states, notably New York, these are very strange indeed and often keep serious, well-known candidates off the ballot.

(6) How to allocate the delegates. In most primaries, candidates are awarded delegates in proportion to the votes they get. This is known as a **proportional primary.** Most states set a **threshold** — a minimum percentage of votes a candidate must receive to get any of that state's delegates. The threshold is often around 10% of the vote. However, in some primaries, whoever gets the most votes wins *all* that state's delegates to the National Party Convention. This is known as a **winner-takes-all primary**. The Democratic Party forbids them, so all their primaries are proportional primaries.

In answers, having quickly made the distinction between primaries and caucuses, you can use the term 'primaries', as that is what the vast majority of states hold nowadays.

In the USA, unlike the UK, you have to take the initiative to go and register to vote.

Notice this is no more than saying you are a Democrat or a Republican. It does not require you to be a paid-up, card-carrying party member.

Again, don't use the term 'proportional representation'. It isn't.

Candidate	Votes	Percentage	Delegates
Al Gore	1,965,716	81.3	304
Bill Bradley	438,010	18.1	63

Table 2.3 A proportional primary: the California Democratic primary, 2000

Candidate	Votes	Percentage	Delegates
George W. Bush	1,542,447	60.6	162
John McCain	885,438	34.8	0
Alan Keyes	100,195	4.0	0

Table 2.4 A winner-takes-all primary: the California Republican primary, 2000

2.4 The growth in importance of primaries

Nowadays the presidential primaries are very important. They are really the only route to becoming the presidential nominee of a major party. But that was not always the case. Until 1968, most states did not hold either primaries or caucuses. Candidates might enter a few or none of the primaries. Decisions were made not by **registered voters in primaries or caucuses** but rather by **state party officials in State Party Conventions**. These were the so-called 'smoke-filled rooms'. They were dominated by important state party officials such as state governors, city mayors or state party chairmen. These were the so-called 'party bosses'. The system was undemocratic and often corrupt.

In 1968, the Democratic presidential nomination went to Vice-President Hubert Humphrey, who had not entered a single primary. Supporters of Senator Eugene McCarthy who had entered a number of that year's 18 Democratic primaries and caucuses were angry. After Humphrey lost the November election, the Democrats set up the **McGovern–Fraser Commission** to draw up new rules for selecting future presidential nominees. This Commission recommended that:

- all states should hold either primaries or caucuses (primaries being preferred, as they are a secret ballot and attract a larger turn-out)
- all delegates should be chosen in these primaries and caucuses
- delegates should be representative — in terms of gender, race and age — of their state parties

This is why they also affected the Republican Party.

These reforms were implemented by **changes in state laws** in readiness for the 1972 presidential election. Ever since then, primaries have grown in number and importance. Nowadays, anyone who wants to be seriously considered for the presidential nomination of either the Democratic or Republican party must enter the primaries and caucuses because it is there that the vast majority of delegates are won. And it is the delegates who finally choose the candidate.

2.5 Front-loading

As primaries have become more and more important, states have tried to make their primary more prominent and influential by moving the date earlier in the year. This is called '**front-loading**'. The number of states holding their primaries or caucuses before the end of March increased from just 11 in 1980 to 36 by 2004. And those 36 states included 7 of the 8 largest states — New York, Texas, California, Florida, Illinois, Michigan and Ohio. California had moved from early June to early March. New York had moved from mid-April to early March. By the end of March 2004, almost 80% of the delegates to the Democratic Convention had already been chosen.

The speed with which George W. Bush won the Republican presidential nomination in 2000 can be seen in Table 2.5. That year, with 2,066 delegates attending the Republican National Convention, 1,034 (50% + 1) were needed to win the party's nomination.

Week ending	Number of delegates for George W. Bush	Number of delegates for John McCain
5 February, 2000	15	11
12 February	27	11
19 February	27	11
26 February	67	96
4 March	170	105
11 March	617	231
18 March	1,093	239

Table 2.5 Delegates won in Republican primaries, February to mid–March 2000

2.6 The invisible primary

This front-loading has increased the importance of another phenomenon — the **invisible primary**. The so-called invisible primary begins almost immediately after the previous presidential election and lasts through to the holding of the first primary and caucus of the election year. It is called 'invisible' because no scheduled event is held during this period. There is therefore nothing to see. It is a time when would-be candidates try to get 'mentioned' in the serious press — newspapers like the *Washington Post* and the *New York Times* — or on television programmes like *The News Hour with Jim Lehrer* on PBS or *Inside Politics* on CNN. It is during this time that candidates will set up exploratory committees and then, eventually, announce formally that they are running for the presidential nomination of their party. It is also an important time for fundraising.

The News Hour with Jim Lehrer is a US equivalent of the BBC's *Newsnight*.

Because the primary season itself is now so short — in 2004 both George W. Bush and John Kerry had made certain of their party's nomination by 2 March — there is no longer any time to build name recognition, momentum and money *during* the primaries. So one has to do it *before* — during the invisible primary.

This means campaigns start much earlier. For example:
- **1960:** Senator John F. Kennedy announced he was running for the presidency on 2 January of that year, **66 days** before the first primary.
- **2004:** Senator John Kerry announced he was running for the presidency **423 days** before the first primary.

There is also much evidence to suggest that this is a most important stage. For example:
- Since 1964, the Republicans have nominated as their candidate the person who was ahead in the opinion polls at the end of the invisible primary on all 11 occasions (see Table 2.6).
- Since 1964, the Democrats have nominated as their candidate the person who was ahead in the opinion polls at the end of the invisible primary on 7 of those 11 occasions (see Table 2.7).

Year	Republican presidential candidate ahead in opinion polls before the New Hampshire primary	Republican candidate eventually nominated for the presidency
1964	Barry Goldwater	Barry Goldwater
1968	Richard Nixon	Richard Nixon
1972	Richard Nixon	Richard Nixon
1976	Gerald Ford	Gerald Ford
1980	Ronald Reagan	Ronald Reagan
1984	Ronald Reagan	Ronald Reagan
1988	George Bush	George Bush
1992	George Bush	George Bush
1996	Bob Dole	Bob Dole
2000	George W. Bush	George W. Bush
2004	George W. Bush	George W. Bush

Table 2.6 Republican presidential candidates: ahead in opinion polls before the New Hampshire primary and eventually nominated, 1964–2004

Year	Democratic presidential candidate ahead in opinion polls before the New Hampshire primary	Democratic candidate eventually nominated for the presidency
1964	Lyndon Johnson	Lyndon Johnson
1968	Lyndon Johnson	Hubert Humphrey
1972	Hubert Humphrey	George McGovern
1976	Jimmy Carter	Jimmy Carter
1980	Jimmy Carter	Jimmy Carter
1984	Walter Mondale	Walter Mondale
1988	Gary Hart	Michael Dukakis
1992	Bill Clinton	Bill Clinton
1996	Bill Clinton	Bill Clinton
2000	Al Gore	Al Gore
2004	Howard Dean	John Kerry

Table 2.7 Democratic presidential candidates: ahead in opinion polls before the New Hampshire primary and eventually nominated, 1964–2004

2.7 Advantages of primaries

The new system of selecting presidential candidates, introduced as a result of the McGovern–Fraser reforms, has a number of advantages:

- Increased level of participation by ordinary voters.
- Increased choice of candidates.
- Opening up of the process to 'outsider' candidates such as Jimmy Carter (1976) and Bill Clinton (1992).
- Removing the power of the party bosses.
- Significantly diminishing opportunities for corruption by doing away with the old 'smoke-filled rooms'.
- Weeding out candidates not up to the gruelling contest, such as Paul Tsongas of Massachusetts in 1992, who had been diagnosed with cancer in the 1980s.

This was certainly the case in some Republican primaries in 2000 when the race between Governor George W. Bush of Texas and Senator John McCain of Arizona was at its peak (see Table 2.8).

State	1996 turnout	2000 turnout	Percentage increase
Michigan	524,161	1,211,106	131
Massachusetts	284,833	495,231	74
New Hampshire	208,938	238,606	14
Ohio	963,422	1,375,101	43
South Carolina	276,741	545,504	97

Table 2.8 Turnout in selected Republican primaries: 1996 and 2000 compared

2.8 Disadvantages of primaries

This reformed system has a number of identifiable disadvantages:

- Turnout is usually low — less than 20% of eligible voters.
- Voters who do vote are unrepresentative of typical general election voters — more elderly, more ideological, better educated and more wealthy.
- It makes the whole selection process far too long, which may discourage some better-qualified candidates from running.
- It is too expensive.
- It is too media-dominated.
- Bitter personal battles can develop, for example George Bush v. Patrick Buchanan in the 1992 Republican primaries.
- It fails to test a number of important presidential qualities.
- It lacks significant input by professional politicians, with too much power being given to ordinary voters — lacks 'peer review'.

2.9 Possible further reform

This welter of criticism has led to a number of calls for further reform. These tend to fall into a number of categories:

- A national primary.
- A series of four regional primaries: the Northeast, the South, the Midwest, the West.
- Further limits on money-raising and spending.
- A pre-primary mini-convention to choose the shortlist of candidates who would then run in the primaries.
- States voting in order of size of population, beginning with the smallest, followed by medium-sized states and finally the largest.

A plan based principally on the latter proposal was debated at the 2000 Republican National Convention but was defeated after George W. Bush let it be known he did not favour such a reform.

The are four problems with these reforms:

(1) The National Committees and Conventions of **both** parties would have to agree to the same reform.

(2) All 50 states would have to agree to change their state laws.

(3) A number of states strongly favour the current system over any of the proposals above.

(4) Limiting money-raising and spending would require an Act of Congress. Up until now there has been little agreement between the two parties on the subject of campaign finance reform.

Use the term 'more ideological' rather than 'extremist'. The latter overstates the point as well as having overtones of disapproval.

Your 'peers' being your 'equals' — those who supposedly know you best.

This would certainly result in the primary season lasting longer than it does at present, because large-population states like California, New York and Texas would not vote until the end of the primary season.

3

National Party Conventions

3.1 The staging of National Party Conventions

Each of the major parties — and some minor parties — hold a National Party Convention. They are:

- held in the summer of the presidential election year (July/August) and usually last for 4 days
- held in a large city: in 2004, Republicans in New York, Democrats in Boston
- held at a venue decided by each party's National Committee
- attended by delegates (most of them chosen in the primaries) and the media

3.2 The formal functions

These Conventions are said to have three **formal** functions:

(1) To choose the presidential candidate.
(2) To choose the vice-presidential candidate.
(3) To decide on the party platform (that is the policy document or 'manifesto').

3.2a Choosing the presidential candidate

This function has been lost almost entirely to the primaries. Almost all of the delegates who attend the Conventions are nowadays chosen in the primaries. They are chosen as 'committed delegates' — committed to voting for their candidate on the first ballot at the Convention if he/she is still in the race.

To win the presidential nomination, a candidate must receive an absolute majority of the delegate votes. In 2004, there were 4,322 delegates attending the Democratic National Convention. John Kerry therefore needed 2,162 votes to win the nomination. Once he had won that number of committed delegates — which as we have already seen he had done by late March — he was the certain nominee of his party, 4 months before the Democratic National Convention met at the end of July.

It is therefore more accurate to state that the Convention merely **confirms** rather than **chooses** the presidential candidate. Not since the Republican Convention of 1976 has the choice of the presidential candidate really been in any doubt at the opening of the Convention. In that year, President Gerald Ford defeated ex-Governor Ronald Reagan by 1,187 delegate votes to 1,070.

3.2b Choosing the vice-presidential candidate

Again, this function has also been lost. Not since 1956 has a National Convention actually chosen the vice-presidential candidate or **running-mate**. Nowadays, the running-mate is chosen by the presidential candidate. Indeed, in recent years the announcement of the running-mate has been made *before* rather than *at* the National Convention. In 2000, both George W. Bush and Al Gore announced their running-mates — Dick Cheney and Joseph Lieberman, respectively — a week before their Conventions convened. In 2004, John Kerry announced his choice of John Edwards 3 weeks before his party's national Convention.

It is therefore more accurate to state that the Convention merely **confirms** rather than **chooses** the vice-presidential candidate.

Avoid the common error of candidates who state that the Conventions 'choose the president' and 'choose the vice-president'. They don't. They choose the presidential and vice-presidential *candidates*.

Don't worry too much about who the delegates are and exactly how they are chosen. Examiners will not expect that level of detail.

In choosing the vice-presidential candidate, the presidential candidate often looks for a **balanced ticket**. This means choosing a running-mate who is different from them in terms of:

- geographic region of origin or residence
- and maybe: gender, race, religion
- political experience
- age

A good example of a 'balanced ticket' would be the Democratic ticket in 1988 of Michael Dukakis and Lloyd Bentsen. This is shown in Table 2.9.

Characteristic	Michael Dukakis	Lloyd Bentsen
Political experience	State Governor	US Congress
Geographic region	Northeast (Massachusetts)	South (Texas)
Race and Religion	Greek-American Greek Orthodox	White, Anglo-Saxon, Protestant (WASP)
Age	54	67
Ideology	liberal Democrat	conservative Democrat

Table 2.9 A balanced ticked: Dukakis–Bentsen, 1988

3.2c Deciding on the party platform

The party platform is the document containing the policies that the party intends to follow if it wins the election. The platform is put together by the **platform committee** under the direction of the party's National Committee. The platform committee holds **hearings** around the country during the first 6 months of the election year. A draft platform is presented to delegates at the beginning of the Convention. There may then be debates on various **planks** — parts of the platform. But nowadays, parties try to avoid heated and contentious debates at the Convention. They feel it makes the party look divided — like the Republican Convention in 1992, in its disagreement over abortion.

The party platform is what is called the 'manifesto' in British politics.

These are known as 'floor fights'.

3.3 The informal functions

The Conventions are said to have three *informal* functions:

- To promote party unity.
- To enthuse the party faithful.
- To enthuse the ordinary voters.

3.3a Promoting party unity

Promoting party unity is a very important function of the Conventions because:

- it is the only time in 4 years that the party actually meets together, during the rest of the time existing merely as 50 state parties
- any wounds created in the primaries can be healed
- it gives the defeated candidates an opportunity to support publicly the chosen candidate (e.g. John McCain supporting George W. Bush at the 2000 Republican Convention and Howard Dean supporting John Kerry at the 2004 Democratic Convention)

The media will comment on whether or not the party is united. Disunited Conventions usually lead to defeat at the general election (e.g. Republicans 1992; Democrats 1980).

3.3b Enthusing the party faithful

Reference to the 'party faithful' means the delegates. It is important that they are 'enthused' by the candidates and the platform because:

* they are the people who will be organising and carrying out much of the campaigning at a state and local level
* they need to communicate that enthusiasm to ordinary voters in their own communities
* they therefore need to believe that they have a winning ticket and winning policies

3.3c Enthusing the ordinary voters

The 'ordinary voters' of course are not at the Convention. It is through television that the parties will hope to communicate with them, and especially through the media coverage of the presidential candidate's **acceptance speech** on the last night of the Convention. This is important because:

* it is the first opportunity for the presidential candidate to address ordinary voters
* the candidate will hope to display presidential qualities to voters
* the candidate will give an outline of the policies to be addressed
* the candidate will hope to boost their opinion poll ratings as a direct result — what is called '**bounce**' (see Table 2.10)

This was especially important for Governor George W. Bush in 2000 because typical American voters knew very little about him. He was the first Republican to win the presidential nomination of his party at the first attempt since Senator Barry Goldwater in 1964.

Year	Challenging party	Bounce	Incumbent party	Bounce
1964	Goldwater (R)	+5	Johnson (D)	+3
1968	Nixon (R)	+5	Humphrey (D)	–7
1972	McGovern (D)	0	Nixon (R)	+7
1976	Carter (D)	+9	Ford (R)	+5
1980	Reagan (R)	+8	Carter (D)	+10
1984	Mondale (D)	+9	Reagan (R)	+4
1988	Dukakis (D)	+7	Bush (R)	+6
1992	Clinton (D)	+16	Bush (R)	+5
1996	Dole (R)	+11	Clinton (D)	+5
2000	Bush (R)	+6	Gore (D)	+7
2004	Kerry (D)	+1	Bush (R)	+4

Note Kerry's almost non-existent bounce in 2004.

Table 2.10 Post-Convention 'bounce', 1964–2004

3.4 The importance of modern-day Conventions

Many commentators suggest that, in comparison to Conventions of years ago, modern-day Conventions are of little importance because:

* the presidential candidates are chosen in the primaries
* the vice-presidential candidates are chosen by the presidential candidates and often announced before the Convention
* the parties try to lay on 'scripted' and 'sanitised' Conventions, devoid of controversy, and hence of interest

- the terrestrial (as opposed to the cable) television companies have given less and less time to the coverage of Conventions

However, Conventions should not be too easily written off. Whilst the formal functions may have declined in importance, the informal functions are still very important. As presidential election scholar Stephen Wayne puts it, the Conventions 'may have become less newsworthy, but they are still important'.

4 The general election campaign

'intra' = within;
'inter' = between.

Labor Day is the US equivalent of the August Bank Holiday in the UK.

The general election:
- is when the **intra-party** campaign has finished and the **inter-party** campaign begins
- by tradition begins on Labor Day — the first Monday in September — but recently has begun straight after the Conventions
- runs for 8–9 weeks until the day before election day in early November
- is very expensive (see Topic 2.C)
- is conducted largely on television (see Topic 2.D)
- includes the televised presidential debates — usually three of the during October — plus one televised debate between the two vice-presidential candidates (see Topic 2.D)

The candidates will tour the country, spending time in states that have large numbers of Electoral College votes and/or which are seen as 'swing' states, that is, could be won by either party.

5 Election day and the Electoral College

5.1 Election day

On election day:
- all registered voters are eligible to vote
- only around 50% of registered voters will vote
- polling stations are open at times decided by state law — usually from 7 or 8 a.m. to 7 or 8 p.m.
- once the polls close, votes are counted in each state
- the television networks will announce results based mostly on exit polls
- the television networks 'award' the Electoral College votes of each state on a winner-takes-all basis and announce the overall winner usually about 4–5 hours after the polls close on the east coast

This is what the television networks got so disastrously wrong over Florida in 2000.

5.2 The Electoral College

5.2a How it works

It is the *number* equal to the state's representation in Congress, not the Senate and House *members* themselves.

Each state is awarded a certain number of Electoral College votes (ECVs). This number is equal to that state's representation in Congress — the number of Senators (2) plus the number of Representatives. Thus in 2004, California had 55 ECVs whilst Wyoming had only 3.

You need to be aware that the apportionment of Electoral College votes in some states altered before the 2004 election.

State	2000 ECVs	2004 ECVs	Change
Arizona	8	10	+2
Florida	25	27	+2
Georgia	13	15	+2
Texas	32	34	+2
California	54	55	+1
Colorado	8	9	+1
Nevada	4	5	+1
North Carolina	14	15	+1
Connecticut	8	7	−1
Illinois	22	21	−1
Indiana	12	11	−1
Michigan	18	17	−1
Mississippi	7	6	−1
Ohio	21	20	−1
Oklahoma	8	7	−1
Wisconsin	11	10	−1
New York	33	31	−2
Pennsylvania	23	21	−2

Table 2.11 Changes in Electoral College votes in 2004: winners and losers

Be careful to get this right. An absolute majority is more than everyone else put together: 50% + 1.

There are a total of 538 ECVs. To win the presidency, a candidate must win an **absolute majority** of ECVs — that is 270.

The popular votes are counted in each state. Whichever candidate wins the most popular votes in a state receives all the ECVs of that state. This is not in the Constitution, but 48 of the 50 states have a state law requiring it. The other two states — Maine and Nebraska — award ECVs on a different basis, depending on who wins the presidential vote in each congressional district.

Don't worry too much about who the Electors actually are. Examiners will not expect you to know that level of detail.

The Electoral College never meets together. The Electors meet in their respective state capitals on the Monday after the second Wednesday in December and send their results to the vice-president in Washington DC.

The vice-president announces the result to a joint session of Congress in early January. If no candidate wins 270 ECVs, the president will be elected by the House of Representatives, with each *state* having one vote — that is a total of 50 votes. The winner would have to receive an absolute majority (26) of those votes. Balloting would continue until this occurred. Meanwhile, the vice-president would be elected by the Senate with each Senator having one vote — that is a total of 100 votes. The winner would need to receive an absolute majority (51) of those votes. Balloting would continue until this occurred. Only twice has the Electoral College failed to come up with a winner and the election been thrown to Congress — 1800 and 1824.

5.2b The strengths of the Electoral College system

However, 3 of the 12 in which the winner has not received at least 50% of the popular vote were 1992, 1996 and 2000 (see Table 2.1).

There are two principal strengths of the Electoral College system:
(1) It preserves the voice of the small-population states.
(2) It promotes a two-horse race, with the winner therefore receiving over 50% of the popular vote, giving the president a mandate to govern. In 24 of the last 36 elections (67%), the winner gained more than 50% of the popular vote.

5.2c The weaknesses of the Electoral College system

However, there are a number of weaknesses associated with the Electoral College system. Amongst them are the following:

(1) Small states are over-represented. This is because every state, regardless of population, has two senators and one House member. Wyoming has three ECVs for its roughly half-a-million people. California has 55 ECVs for its over 30 million. Thus, although California has over 60 times as many people, it gets only 18 times as many ECVs as Wyoming. If California had ECVs on the same basis as Wyoming, it should have 180 of them!

(2) The winner-takes-all system can distort the result. In 1996, Clinton won 49% of the popular vote but 70% of the ECVs.

(3) It is possible for a candidate to win the overall popular vote throughout the 50 states but lose in the Electoral College. This occurred in 2000 when Gore polled just under 540,000 more votes nationwide than Bush but lost 271–266 in the Electoral College. This has occurred twice before, in 1876 and 1888, and almost occurred in 1960 and 1968 (see Table 2.12).

Year	Candidates	Popular vote percentage	Electoral College votes
1876	Samuel Tilden (D)	51.0	184
	Rutherford Hayes (R)	47.9	185
1888	Grover Cleveland (D)	48.6	168
	Benjamin Harrison (R)	47.8	233
1960	**John Kennedy (D)**	49.8	303
	Richard Nixon (R)	49.5	219
1968	**Richard Nixon (R)**	43.2	301
	Hubert Humphrey (D)	42.7	191
	George Wallace (I)	13.5	46
2000	Al Gore (D)	48.4	266
	George W. Bush (R)	47.9	271

Table 2.12 Presidential elections: selected results (winners in bold)

(4) It is very unfair to **national** third parties. In 1992, Ross Perot gained 19% of the popular vote but won no ECVs.

Year	State	Number of Electors	Elector should have voted for	Elector actually voted for
1960	Alabama	6	John Kennedy	Harry Byrd
	Mississippi	8	John Kennedy	Harry Byrd
	Oklahoma	1	Richard Nixon	Harry Byrd
1968	North Carolina	1	Richard Nixon	George Wallace
1972	Virginia	1	Richard Nixon	John Hospers
1976	Washington	1	Gerald Ford	Ronald Reagan
1988	West Virginia	1	Michael Dukakis	Lloyd Bentsen
2000	Washington DC	1	Al Gore	No-one

Table 2.13 'Rogue Electors', 1960–2000

(5) So-called 'rogue' or 'faithless' Electors vote for candidates other than the one who won the popular vote in their state (see Table 2.13).

(6) The system used in the case of an Electoral College deadlock could result in

Not the case in 2004.

It should have been 271–267 but one Elector from Washington DC refused to cast her vote for Al Gore in protest against the city's lack of representation in Congress.

It is important to say 'national' third parties, as 'regional' third parties — such as George Wallace's Independent Party in 1968 — can win Electoral College votes more easily.

the House choosing a president of one party and the Senate choosing a vice-president of another party.

5.2d Possible reforms of the Electoral College system

Here are three possible reforms of the Electoral College system:

(1) Abandon the winner-takes-all system for **a more proportional system** (already used by two states — Maine and Nebraska). Had Florida been using a proportional system in 2000, it might have eased the problem. Instead of deciding who was going to get 25 ECVs and who was going to get none, it might have instead decided who got 13 ECVs and who got 12.

(2) Pass state laws to **prohibit 'rogue' Electors** from casting such rogue votes.

(3) Abolish the Electoral College altogether and decide the election on the popular vote. The problem with that is it would encourage a multi-candidate election with the winner gaining maybe only 35–40% of the votes.

> But remember: all reforms require either changes in state laws or a constitutional amendment. Both are very difficult to achieve and therefore unlikely.

B Voting behaviour

The subject of voting behaviour attempts to answer these kinds of questions about why people vote as they do:

- How important is party affiliation?
- Are there differences in the voting habits of men and women?
- How important is race in voting?
- What about religious groups?
- What about the voting habits of the poor as opposed to the better-off?
- Does geographic region have anything to tell us?
- What role do policies play?

1 Party affiliation

Despite all we say about political parties being not all that important in US politics, party affiliation seems to be an important ingredient in determining voting. In the 2004 presidential election:

- 74% of voters identified with one of the two major parties: 37% called themselves Democrats; 37% called themselves Republicans
- 89% of the Democrats voted for Kerry
- 93% of the Republicans voted for Bush

In the presidential elections between 1952 and 2004, the party that managed to gain the highest level of support from its own identifiers won on 12 out of 14 occasions.

Winning elections is as much about **mobilising** your own supporters as it is about **converting** supporters of your opponent so that they vote for you. It is also about who manages to get people to the voting booths on election day. Do your supporters turn out or stay at home? Elections are determined just as much by the stay-at-homes as by those who turn up to vote.

This is what is called the 'gender gap'.

However, Catholics, who tended to vote Democratic, may not follow this trend. Also note that Bush won the majority of Catholic votes in 2004, against a Democratic candidate who was a Catholic.

2 *Gender*

With regards to gender and voting, the following points are worth noting:

- Women are more likely to be registered voters than men.
- Women tend to turn out in higher numbers on election day than men.
- In recent elections, the trend has been for men to be more supportive of Republican candidates whilst women have tended to support the Democrats.
- In the presidential elections between 1964 and 2004, women were more supportive than men of the Democrats in 10 out of 11 elections.
- Women are more likely to be registered Democrats than registered Republicans.

The reasons for this are thought to derive from the stance of the two major parties on such policies as:

- **abortion** — Democrats tend to be pro-choice and Republicans tend to be pro-life
- **defence** — women tend to favour lower levels of spending, the Democrats' position
- **law and order** — women tend to oppose capital punishment, again the Democrats' position
- **gun control** — women tend to support this, another Democrat position
- **women's rights** — Democrats supported the Equal Rights Amendment; Republicans tended to oppose it.

So, to win elections, the Republicans are always looking for ways to appeal more to women voters, whilst Democrats are trying to attract more male voters. And because there are more women than men amongst registered voters, the larger the turnout, the better it is for the Democrats.

Category	% of electorate	Bush (%)	Kerry (%)
All	100	51	48
Democrats	37	11	89
Republicans	37	93	6
Independents	26	48	49
Men	51	55	44
Women	49	48	51
White men	36	61	38
White women	41	55	45
Black men	5	13	86
Black women	7	10	90
Protestant	54	59	40
Catholic	27	52	47
Jewish	3	25	74
Family income:			
Under $15,000	8	36	63
$15,000–$29,999	15	42	57
$30,000–$49,999	22	49	50
$50,000–$74,999	23	56	43
Over $75,000	32	57	42
East	22	43	56
South	32	58	42
West	20	49	50
Midwest	26	51	48

Table 2.14 Who voted for whom, 2004

3 Race

3.1 African-Americans

African-Americans, who make up some 10% of the US electorate, have since the 1960s given solid support to the Democratic Party. Traditionally, the Republicans — 'the party of Lincoln' — had thought of the black vote as theirs, following Lincoln's freeing of the slaves after the Civil War. But that changed during the twentieth century for two reasons. First, it was Democrat Franklin Roosevelt's 'New Deal' that helped out-of-work and poor African-Americans in the 1930s. Second, Democrats Kennedy and Johnson got Congress to pass civil rights laws that protected the rights of African-Americans in such matters as housing, education, employment and voting. In the six presidential elections since 1980, African-Americans never gave less than 83% support to the Democrat candidate. In 2004, it was 88%.

3.2 Hispanics

Hispanics are a more diverse group and encompass:
- Cuban-Americans
- Puerto Rican-Americans
- Mexican-Americans
- those from other Central American countries

But they are a numerically growing group. Hence their importance increases at each election.

Cuban-Americans, especially those in South Florida, have tended to support Republican candidates. Other Hispanic groups, such as those in California and New Mexico, have tended to support Democrats.

In the 2000 and 2004 elections, the Republicans were seen courting the Hispanic vote. In 1992, George Bush won 24% of the Hispanic vote. In 1996, it dropped to 20% for Bob Dole. But by 2004 it was 43% for George W. Bush.

4 Religion

There are certain trends in voting according to religion, a factor much stronger in US politics than in the UK. Note the following four points:

(1) **Protestant voters tend to vote Republican.** They didn't give Clinton a majority of their votes in either 1992 or 1996 — they went for Bush in 1992 (45%–34%) and for Dole in 1996 (47%–43%). In 2004, they broke in favour of George W. Bush (59%–40%).

(2) **Catholic voters tend to vote Democrat**, though not as strongly as used to be the case. But they did give Clinton a 54%–37% vote in 1992 and 42%–37% in 1996. The Democrats' pro-choice position on abortion can be a liability with Catholic voters. But in 2004, Bush won the majority of Catholic voters — 52%–47%.

(3) **Jewish voters tend to vote Democrat** pretty solidly. (But they make up only 3% of the electorate.) They gave Clinton 78% support in both 1992 and 1996. They have given a majority of their votes to the Democrat candidate in every presidential election since the Second World War. In 2000, they gave 79% support

Presidential elections

to the Gore–Lieberman ticket. So Al Gore's choice of Joseph Lieberman — an orthodox Jew — as his running-mate in 2000 did not obviously help him politically with Jews.

(4) In the 2000 presidential election, there was **a high correlation between attendance at religious services and voting Republican**, as shown in Table 2.15. Of those voters who attend religious services weekly or more than weekly — and that was 42% of all voters — 63% voted for George W. Bush.

The figure in the UK is 8%!

Attend religious services	% of electorate	Bush (%)	Gore (%)	Nader (%)
More than weekly	14	63	36	1
Weekly	28	57	40	2
Monthly	14	46	51	2
Seldom	28	42	54	3
Never	14	32	61	6

Table 2.15 Frequency of attendance at religious services and candidate support, 2000

5 Wealth

There is a strong correlation between relative wealth and likely support of the two major parties. In both 1992 and 1996, Clinton had his highest support amongst those earning under $15,000 (£10,000) a year and his lowest support amongst those earning over $100,00 (£66,000) a year. Likewise, in both elections, the Republicans received their lowest support among the poorest and their highest support among the most wealthy. The pattern was repeated in 2004, with Kerry winning 63% of the poorest voters but only 41% of the wealthiest, whilst Bush won only 36% of the poorest voters but 58% of the wealthiest.

6 Geographic region

There are certain trends in voting according to geographic region. Consider the following four points:

(1) **The Northeast tends to support the Democrats.** The region's big cities gave Bill Clinton his highest level of support in any region in both 1992 and 1996 and likewise for Gore in 2000 and Kerry in 2004. Bad news for the Democrats — demographically, the Northeast is a declining region. Fewer people means less political clout.

For example Boston, New York, Philadelphia, Baltimore.

(2) From the end of the Civil War in the 1860s until the 1960s, the South was described as 'the solid South' — voting solidly for the Democratic Party. The rule was simply 'vote as you shot'. But in the last three decades of the twentieth century **the 'solid south' for the Democrats has collapsed.** The South voted for Bush in 1992, Dole in 1996 and George W. Bush in 2000 and 2004 — the only region in each election to vote Republican. Good news for the Republicans — demographically the South is a growing region. More people means more political clout.

'Vote as you shot' means that if your family shot for the Confederate South in the Civil War then you still voted for the party of the South — the Democrats.

(3) **The West tends to support the Democrats.** States such as California, Oregon, Washington voted solidly for Clinton in 1992 and 1996, although Green Party

candidate Ralph Nader nibbled away at Gore's majority in the Pacific Northwest in 2000. Kerry won all three west coast states in 2004.

(4) The Midwest is the battle-ground in modern elections. Since 1960, whoever wins Missouri wins the White House — true now of the last 12 presidential elections. In 2000, the Midwest broke 49%–48% between Bush and Gore. Nationally it was 48%–48%. In 2004, the Midwest broke 51%–48% between Bush and Kerry, exactly the same as the national vote. Today's presidential elections are largely won and lost in Missouri (Bush won by 7 percentage points in 2004), Michigan (Kerry won by 3 points) and Ohio (Bush won by 2 points).

7 Policies

A sign bearing this slogan hung in the Clinton campaign head-quarters as the answer to the question: 'What is the main issue of this election?'

Policies matter. But which ones? They can easily change from one election to another. Here are four important points to note about policies and voting:

(1) In the **1992** election, it was 'the economy, stupid!' In that election, voters who thought the economy was in 'good shape' voted 82% for George Bush, whilst those who thought it in 'poor shape' voted 65% for Clinton. The trouble for Bush was that twice as many voters fell into the second category as into the first.

(2) In **1992**, Bush also suffered from the fact that in an election in which he was trumpeting his foreign policy successes — most notably, victory in the Persian Gulf War — only 8% of voters thought that foreign policy mattered as an issue. That figure had been 23% back in 1988 when Bush was elected.

(3) In **2000**, the four issues most frequently mentioned by voters as being those that mattered were: the economy and jobs; education; social security; taxes. But voters preferred Gore's position on the first three. Only on taxes did Bush have a majority who preferred his policies — but it was 80%–17%! (See Table 2.16.)

(4) In **2004**, the four main issues were 'moral values', the economy/jobs, terrorism and Iraq.

Which issues mattered most in deciding your vote?	% of electorate	Bush (%)	Kerry (%)
Moral values	22	80	18
Economy/jobs	20	18	80
Terrorism	19	86	14
Iraq	15	26	73
Taxes	5	57	43
Education	4	26	73

Table 2.16 Issues and voting, 2004

8 Conclusions

This refers to a coalition including urban workers, racial minorities, farmers, southerners and liberals.

- The old Democrat '**New Deal coalition**' has weakened.
- During the 1990s, Bill Clinton tried to move the Democratic Party away from its old 'tax and spend', liberal base to a more centrist 'third way'.
- The Democrats have lost significant support amongst Southern whites and have a problem attracting male voters, but they are still very strong in the Northeast.

- The Republicans have experienced difficulties attracting women voters and those of racial minorities but they are very strong amongst white, evangelical Christians and in the so-called 'sun-belt' states.
- Typical Democrat voting blocs: blue-collar, unionised workers; urban dwellers; West and Northeast; Jewish; racial minority, possibly black; female; liberal; less wealthy; less well-educated.
- Typical Republican voting blocs: white-collar, professional workers; suburban and rural; sun-belt; Protestant, especially evangelical and increasingly Catholic; white and increasingly Hispanic; male; conservative; well-off; college-educated.

C Money

1 Pre-reforms

US election campaigns are often criticised for spending vast sums of money. Such criticism may well have merit, but it is important to remember some of the reasons why US elections are so expensive, especially when compared with UK parliamentary elections:
- The country is vast (the entire UK is the size of Oregon).
- The elections are not just to elect one legislative chamber (as in the UK).
- The general election campaign lasts 9 weeks, not 3–4 weeks as in the UK.
- Candidates must contest the primaries, which begin 9 months before election day.
- There is no 'free time' on US television; buying time is expensive.

Until the 1970s, campaign finance was largely unregulated, which meant that:
- personal wealth was important in running for political office (e.g. JFK in 1960)
- people were not limited in the sums they could give to candidates
- '**fat cats**' gave huge sums (often running into millions of dollars) to candidates
- candidates were not limited in the sums they could spend on their campaigns
- many opportunities for corruption existed

Be careful when writing about the importance of money. It is misleading to say that someone 'needs a lot of money' to run for the presidency. That could be taken to mean that you have to be personally wealthy. Say, rather, that someone 'needs *to raise a lot of money*' to run for the presidency.

2 The 1970s reforms

A number of events occurred in the 1970s that led to a different system of campaign finance:
- Congress began to pass legislation in 1971 to restrict campaign contributions and expenditure.
- The Watergate affair acted as a catalyst for change.
- Congress passed another campaign finance law in 1974.

The Federal Election Campaign Act (1974):
- limited individual contributions to a candidate to $1,000
- limited corporate contributions to a candidate to $5,000
- forbade donations from foreign donors
- limited candidates' expenditure to $10 million (1974) in the primaries and

a further $20 million (1974) in the general election — these figures to be index-linked for inflation every 4 years

Don't confuse this with the 'matching funds' given by the federal government to states to help them provide certain services.

- provided for '**matching funds**' from the federal tax payer to help finance presidential elections
- established the **Federal Election Commission** (FEC) to enforce and regulate this new system

3 The 2002 reforms

But the 1970s reforms left a number of loopholes which became new and significant problems during the elections of the 1980s and 1990s. These included problems concerning:
- 'Soft money' spent by political parties on 'party building' or 'get-out-the-vote' activities.
- The growth in 'issue advocacy' campaigning by, for example, abortion, environmental and labour union groups.
- The weakening of the political parties as 'matching funds' went directly to the candidates' organisations rather than to the parties.
- The failure of the Federal Election Commission to have much in the way of enforcement powers against those who broke the new rules.

Following the campaign finance abuses surrounding Bill Clinton's re-election campaign, Republican Senator John McCain made campaign finance reform a key issue in his (eventually unsuccessful) campaign for the Republican presidential nomination in 2000. But eventually, along with Democrat Senator Russell Feingold, he was successful in getting another raft of reforms passed through Congress in 2002.

The principal changes brought about by the 2002 reforms were:
- National Party Committees banned from raising or spending 'soft money'.
- Labour unions and corporate groups forbidden from directly funding issue advertisements.
- The banning of union or corporate money to fund advertisements that mention a federal candidate, within 60 days of a general election or 30 days of a primary.
- The prohibition of fundraising on federal property.

D The media

The term 'the media' includes print journalism, radio and television, though the latter is the most important in this context.

1 Newspapers

There are no national titles, except for *USA Today* (a weekday broadsheet) and the *Wall Street Journal* (the US equivalent of the UK's *Financial Times*). But there are

local papers that have a national reputation, such as the *Washington Post* and the *New York Times*. What is most important is what these kinds of papers say on their 'op–ed' (short for 'opinion–editorial') pages as well as the endorsements they make of particular candidates near to election day. Don't forget also the websites that these and other newspapers now maintain.

For example:
www.washingtonpost.com,
www.nytimes.com,
www.washtimes.com

2 Journals

These are weeklies aimed at a general readership. The main titles are *Time* and *Newsweek*, but *US News and World Report* is in the same market, though aimed at a more specifically political audience. 'Cover stories' are the most important factor of these journals, that is the inside story which features on the cover of that week's edition. Again, related websites are now used extensively.

3 Television

3.1 Different types and forms of television

Television is the principal medium for imparting information during a US election. It exists in two forms:
(1) Terrestrial — the 'networks': ABC, CBS, NBC and PBS.
(2) Cable: CNN, Fox News, MSNBC, C-SPAN.

Also good websites —
for example
www.abcnews.com,
www.cnn.com

Television carries mainly three different forms of political information and coverage:
(1) Daily news programmes: e.g. ABC's *Good Morning America* and *World News Tonight*.
(2) Nightly/weekly documentary programmes: e.g. *The News Hour with Jim Lehrer* (PBS), *Inside Politics* (CNN), *The McLaughlin Group* (NBC), which will contain serious political interviews.
(3) Chat shows: e.g. *Larry King Live* (CNN).

3.2 The televised presidential debates

There are now the traditional televised presidential debates during the general election campaign. These began in 1960 between Kennedy and Nixon, but were not used again until 1976 between Ford and Carter. They have been used in every election year since then. There are usually three presidential and one vice-presidential debate, each lasting $1\frac{1}{2}$ hours. They generally include only Democrat and Republican candidates, though Ross Perot and his running-mate James Stockdale were included in 1992. Most have been in the format of a joint press conference with a panel of journalists asking questions. But from 1992, 'town hall' style debates have also been used — a more informal style with questions put by an invited audience.

In this sense they are
not really 'debates' at
all, as there is no
communication
between the candidates.

These debates can be important. The following rules of thumb should be noted:
(1) Style is often more important than substance — it's not what you say, but how you say it and how you look.
(2) Avoid serious gaffes.
(3) Look for opportunities to deliver a 'sound bite' that will be used by the news organisations in their 'highlights'.

For example, Bush having to defend breaking his 1988 'No New Taxes' pledge in the 1992 debates with Clinton.

(4) Debates are more difficult for incumbent presidents than for challengers because incumbents have a record to defend and can have their words from 4 years ago quoted back at them.

3.3 Television commercials

Television commercials date from the 1952 campaign. They are usually 30-second commercials, but may be longer nearer election day.

There are different types of commercials. There are those that are **positive** about your candidate. These may be either **biographical** or **policy-orientated**. There are also **negative** commercials, talking only about your opponent. These may be either **'attack ads'** or **humorous** — attempting to poke fun at one's opponent.

For example, the 'Willie Horton' commercial used by Bush against Dukakis in 1988 may have hurt Bush as much as Dukakis.

Discussion regarding television commercials centres upon:
● cost
● whether 'attack ads' are double-edged swords, which hurt the purveyor more than the intended target
● the extent to which commercials change voters' minds and voting intentions
● evidence that commercials do little in the way of **'conversion'** but more in terms of **'reinforcement'** and **'activation'** — reinforcing what voters already think and activating them to turn out and vote for your candidate

3.4 Television at the National Conventions

There is plenty of evidence to show that there is much less coverage of the National Party Conventions than was the case in the 1960s. There are two principal reasons for this:
(1) The Conventions are no longer actually choosing the presidential candidates.
(2) The advent of cable television means that viewers can switch away from coverage on the terrestrial channels.

There has been criticism of the terrestrial networks (ABC, CBS, NBC) that they are not fulfilling their 'public service' by failing to give full coverage to the Conventions.

Day	ABC	CBS	NBC	Total
Day 1	1968: $1\frac{1}{2}$ hours 2000: 1 hour	1968: $6\frac{1}{2}$ hours 2000: 0	1968: $7\frac{1}{2}$ hours 2000: 0	1968: $15\frac{1}{2}$ hours 2000: 1 hour
Day 2	1968: $1\frac{1}{2}$ hours 2000: 1 hour	1968: $3\frac{1}{2}$ hours 2000: 0	1968: $4\frac{1}{2}$ hours 2000: 0	1968: $9\frac{1}{2}$ hours 2000: 1 hours
Day 3	1968: $1\frac{1}{2}$ hours 2000: 1 hour	1968: $3\frac{1}{2}$ hours 2000: 1 hour	1968: $6\frac{1}{2}$ hours 2000: 1 hour	1968: $11\frac{1}{2}$ hours 2000: 3 hours
Day 4	1968: $1\frac{1}{2}$ hours 2000: 2 hours	1968: $3\frac{1}{2}$ hours 2000: 2 hours	1968: $4\frac{1}{2}$ hours 2000: $1\frac{1}{2}$ hours	1968: $9\frac{1}{2}$ hours 2000: $5\frac{1}{2}$ hours
Totals	1968: 6 hours 2000: 5 hours	1968: 17 hours 2000: 3 hours	1968: 23 hours 2000: $2\frac{1}{2}$ hours	1968: 46 hours 2000: $10\frac{1}{2}$ hours

Table 2.17 Network television coverage of National Party Conventions: 1968 and 2000 compared

3.5 Television on election night

The controversy concerning the television networks' 'calling' of Florida on election night in 2000 will reverberate for some time to come. Just 35 minutes after the polls closed in most — though not all — of Florida, CNN 'called' Florida for Al Gore, awarding him its 25 Electoral College votes. But less than 3 hours later, it was all change as the networks decided Florida was 'too close to call' and removed 25 Electoral College votes from Gore's total. Three hours later, the networks awarded the state to Bush, only to retract again within the hour, putting the state in the 'too-close-to-call' column yet again — where it remained for 5 weeks!

In 2004, the election night controversy centred on misleading exit poll data.

Amongst the questions raised are:
(1) How reliable is the polling data upon which television networks base their 'predictions'?
(2) Should the television networks wait for all the votes to be counted and announce only actual results, as occurs in UK elections?
(3) Did the television networks affect the result of the 2000 election? Did the early awarding of Florida to Gore discourage would-be Bush voters from turning out in the northwestern part of the state where polls remained open for a further half-an-hour? Did the networks' awarding of the state — and with it the election — to Bush later on give Bush the advantage of appearing as the winner throughout the period of the Court battles in November and December?

Political parties are, of course, important in any democracy. But in the USA they are less important than in many other democracies. They are less important than they are, for example, in the UK. First, the USA is so vast that organising a political party across the length and breadth of the country is rather different from organising a party in the UK. In the USA, as we shall see, parties are more state-based than national. Second, elections in the USA have become much more candidate-centred affairs than they tend to be in the UK, where voters still have quite strong national party ties. In the UK, many people will vote 'Labour' or 'Conservative'. In the USA, people will tend to vote 'Bush' or 'Gore' — or whoever.

The topic is divided into three major headings:

A Party organisation, philosophy and ideology
B The two-party system
C Third parties

A Party organisation, philosophy and ideology

1 *National organisation*

The USA has a federal system of government (see Topic 1.E). Federalism is a decentralised form of government. Some powers are vested in the national government, but other equally important powers are vested in the state governments. The more centralised the government, the more centralised the party system. The less centralised the government, the less centralised the party system. Thus, US political parties are **decentralised**. To be sure, there is some national organisation; but it does not amount to very much. US political parties are principally state-based.

In the USA, the Republican Party is often referred to as the GOP — 'The Grand Old Party'.

The two major US parties — the Democrats and the Republicans — do have something of a national party organisation, but it is fairly limited. Each has a National Committee. The Democratic National Committee (DNC) and the Republican National Committee (RNC) are each headed by a party chairperson. He or she acts as a spokesperson for the national party, especially in the media, and is responsible for the day-to-day running of the party. Although the DNC and RNC meet in full session only twice a year, they are permanent organisations with offices in Washington DC. And, of course, each party holds a National Convention once every 4 years (see Topic 2.A.3). But that is about it.

2 *State organisation*

Everything else is done at the state or local level. At that level, the organisation of each party looks something like this:

- State Party Convention
- State Party Committee (headed by State Party Chairperson)
- County Committees
- District Committees
- City Committees
- Ward Committees
- Precinct Committees

In essays, make a comparison with the very different situation in UK parties.

So it is worth noting that US political parties really have no one who can truly be called the 'party leader'. The president might be said to be 'the leader' of the party. But even that does not mean very much. The party not in control of the White House does not even have that level of national leadership. Except for the period — once every 4 years — between the National Party Convention and the holding of the presidential election, when both parties do have someone who maybe looks and sounds like a national leader, US national political parties are pretty leaderless.

3 *Philosophy and ideology*

In terms of philosophy and ideology, both major parties in the USA are quite diverse. The Democratic Party is usually associated with being the more liberal of the two parties. Yet Democrats come in many shades — 'liberal Democrats', 'moderate Democrats', 'New Democrats' and even 'conservative Democrats'.

It is important to use correctly the words 'conservative' (i.e. the adjective) and 'Conservative' (i.e. the name of a party).

The Republican Party is normally thought of as being the more conservative of the two parties. Yet there are 'moderate Republicans', 'right-wing Republicans', 'Christian conservatives' and, more recently, 'compassionate conservatives'. ('Compassionate conservative' was popularised as a term by George W. Bush in the 2000 election.)

In the 1960s, the Democratic Party contained both 'liberal Democrats' (like President John Kennedy and his brothers senators Robert and Edward Kennedy, pushing for civil rights for African-Americans) and 'conservative Democrats' (like Governor George Wallace of Alabama whom many would have regarded as an unreformed racist).

Even today, the Republican Party contains a huge spectrum of opinion, from a 'conservative Republican' like Senator Trent Lott of Mississippi to a 'moderate Republican' like Senator Olympia Snowe of Maine. Meanwhile, the Democratic Party contains 'liberals' like Senator Barbara Boxer of California on the one hand and 'conservatives' like Senator Blanche Lincoln of Arkansas on the other.

The key to understanding much of this is geography. In the Northeast — in states like New York, Massachusetts or Maine — one will tend to find 'liberal Democrats' and 'moderate Republicans'. The same on the west coast — in states such as California or Oregon. But in the South — in states like Louisiana, Alabama, North and South Carolina — you will tend to come across 'conservative Democrats' and 'conservative Republicans'. Both parties take on different ideological colours from region to region. If they didn't, they wouldn't be national parties. And if they weren't national parties, they wouldn't win the presidency — the greatest prize of US politics.

There was a time was when the southern states were referred to as the **'solid South'**. This was because voters in the South voted solidly for the Democratic Party. This was a consequence of the Civil War, fought in the 1860s. During the Civil War, the Republicans were thought of as the party of the North, the Democrats as the party of the South. And for a century and more later, people in the South would use the slogan **'vote as you shot'**. It wasn't until quite recently, as is shown in Table 3.1, that the South became part of the competitive two-party system.

Year	House: Democrats–Republicans	Senate: Democrats–Republicans	Governors: Democrats–Republicans
1960	99–7	22–0	11–0
1962	95–11	21–1	11–0
1964	89–17	21–1	11–0
1966	83–23	19–3	9–2
1968	80–26	18–4	9–2
1970	79–27	16–5	9–2
1972	77–31	14–7	8–3
1974	81–27	15–6	8–3
1976	80–28	16–5	9–2
1978	78–30	15–6	8–3
1980	69–39	11–10	6–5
1982	82–34	11–11	9–2
1984	80–36	12–10	8–3
1986	78–38	16–6	6–5
1988	77–39	15–7	6–5
1990	77–39	15–7	8–3
1992	77–48	13–9	8–3
1994	61–64	9–13	5–6
1996	54–71	7–15	5–6
1998	54–71	8–14	4–7
2000	53–71	9–13	5–6
2002	55–76	9–13	4–7
2004	49–82	4–18	4–7

Table 3.1 The break-up of the 'solid South', 1960–2004

B The two-party system

1 *The facts*

That the USA does have a two-party system is almost indisputable. Look at the following facts:
- Every president since 1856 has been either a Democrat or a Republican.
- In every presidential election since 1916, the combined Democrat and Republican vote has exceeded 80% of the total votes cast.
- In 19 of those last 23 presidential elections the combined Democrat and Republican vote has exceeded 90% of the total votes cast, reaching 99% in both 1984 and 1988.

In the 2005 UK general election, the combined Labour and Conservative vote was just 67.5%.

Following the 2005 UK general election, there were 91 members of the House of Commons (out of 646) who belonged to neither of the two major parties.

- In January 2005, every member of the US Senate belonged to one of the two major parties, except Senator James Jeffords of Vermont who sits as an Independent.
- At the same time, of the 435 members of the House of Representatives, only 1 is not either a Democrat or a Republican.
- Of the 50 state governors, all are either Democrats or Republicans.

The Democrats and Republicans dominate politics and elections in the USA to a startling extent.

2 The reasons

There are two main reasons why the USA has a two-party system:

(1) The first-past-the-post, winner-takes-all electoral system.

(2) The diversity and all-embracing nature of the two major parties, which allows very little room for third parties.

But it could be argued that the USA does *not* have a two-party system, or that at least the picture is rather more complex than the statistics above would lead us to believe. Consider other analyses of the US party system.

3 Other analyses

Also sometimes referred to as a '100-party system'.

Some commentators have suggested that the USA does not have a two-party system but **a fifty-party system**. Each individual state has its own party system.

Another analysis suggests that some states appear to have a **one-party system**. In such states, one party dominates to such an extent that the other seems hardly to exist. For example, Massachusetts is dominated by the Democratic Party. The Republicans have won the state in only one presidential election in the last 40 years, Reagan winning it by just 3,000 votes out of $2\frac{1}{2}$ million in 1980. In Wyoming, it is the Republicans who in that same period have won all bar one presidential election (1964) and dominate the state at all levels.

Yet another analysis suggests that because of the decline in the importance of political parties, the USA might be said to have a **no-party system**. Let us consider this a little more closely.

4 Theories of party decline

It was David Broder who popularised the idea that political parties in the USA were in serious decline. In the 1970s, he published a book with the title *The Party's Over*. Broder and others have put forward a number of reasons for concluding that the USA's parties were in serious decline:

- **Parties have lost control over presidential candidate selection.** With the rise in importance of presidential primaries (see Topic 2.A.2), parties no longer choose the candidates. This is now done by ordinary voters in the primaries.

- **Parties have been bypassed by federal 'matching funds' in presidential elections.** The 'matching funds' — introduced in the mid-1970s — are given to the candidates, not the parties (see Topic 2.C).
- **Television and opinion polls have bypassed parties as the medium by which candidates communicate with voters.** Party rallies and party-organised 'torch-light' processions etc. were the traditional way in which candidates spoke to and heard from voters. The party was therefore the most important vehicle of communication between politicians and voters. Nowadays, politicians increasingly talk to voters through the medium of television and voters 'talk back' through opinion polls.
- **Campaigns are more candidate-centred and issue-centred than they were.** Voters tend to vote more for a particular candidate, or because a candidate holds a certain view on a particular issue of importance to the voter (e.g. abortion, the environment, gun control), than for the party label. This has also shown itself in the rise of **'split-ticket' voting** (voting for candidates of different parties for different offices at the same election) and of 'independent' voters.

5 *Theories of party renewal*

More recently, however, many commentators have been arguing that American political parties are undergoing renewal. What are the pointers to the theories of party renewal?

- **The party decline theories are somewhat exaggerated.** When all is said and done, it is still true that at the end of the twentieth century all the presidents elected in that century were either Democrats or Republicans; virtually all members of Congress were either Democrats or Republicans; even at the state level, the vast majority of state governors and state legislators were either Democrats or Republicans.
- **The parties have fought to regain some control over the presidential candidate selection process.** The Democratic Party introduced **super delegates** at their 1984 National Convention. These are professional, elected politicians who are given a vote at the Convention *ex officio*. By 2004, these super delegates accounted for almost 20% of the delegate votes at the Democratic National Convention. In 2000, it was possible to see how the choice of the Republican Party 'establishment' — Governor George W. Bush — triumphed over the preferred choice of a significant number of rank-and-file Republican voters — Senator John McCain. The fact that Governor Bush enjoyed the almost unanimous support of the Republican Party hierarchy still counted for a lot even in a system dominated by presidential primaries.

The Brock Reforms were named after Republican National Committee chairman Bill Brock.

- **Both parties have made significant strides in modernising their national party structures and network.** For the Republicans, the **Brock Reforms** significantly strengthened the standing of the Republican National Committee from the 1980s. And in the 1990s, Democratic National Committee chairman Charles Manatt did much the same for the Democrats developing computerised direct mail facilities and a permanent headquarters in Washington DC.
- **The growth of 'soft money' in the 1980s and 1990s.** In an attempt to overcome the negative effects of 'matching funds' going directly to candidates rather than

Soft money can be defined as largely un-regulated money given to national parties for such things as voter registration drives, the commissioning of opinion polls and issue-centred advertising.

the parties, both major parties during the 1980s and 1990s took to raising large sums of 'soft money' which was entirely unregulated and led to new abuses. 'Soft money' was eventually banned by the Campaign Finance Reform Act (2002) known as the McCain–Feingold Act. (See Topic 2.C.3.)

- **Moves towards the 'nationalising' of campaigns.** Not only has this been seen increasingly in presidential elections, but it was also seen very dramatically in the 1994 mid-term congressional elections when the Republican Party launched its **Contract with America**. The brainchild of then Congressman Newt Gingrich, nearly all Republican House candidates in that election signed up to this ten-point contract. It promised, under a Republican-controlled Congress, that votes would be held within the first one hundred days of such a Congress on ten policy issues of interest to conservative voters such as a balanced budget amendment and congressional term limits.

For more details on 'party votes', see Topic 5.G.1.

- **Increased partisanship in Congress.** There has been some evidence that the 1990s saw increased levels of partisanship in Washington DC, especially during the Clinton administration. In 1995, the votes in Congress which were 'party votes' reached 73% in the House of Representatives, the highest figure since 1910. In the Senate the same year, 69% of votes were 'party votes', the highest since 1922. This came to a crescendo during the impeachment and trial of the President in 1998 and early 1999. The votes in the House of Representatives on the Articles of Impeachment were largely along party lines. Article I, accusing the President of perjury, was passed by 228 votes to 206. Only five Democrats voted 'yes' and only five Republicans voted 'no'. When this same Article was voted on in the Senate, the vote was 45 to 55. All those 45 senators voting 'guilty' on Article I were Republicans.

C Third parties

1 Types of third parties

There are a number of different types of third parties in the USA:
- National (e.g. Reform Party, Green Party, Libertarian Party, Natural Law Party).
- Regional (e.g. George Wallace's American Independent Party — 1968).
- State (e.g. New York Conservative Party).
- Permanent (e.g. Green Party, Libertarian Party).
- Temporary (e.g. American Independent Party, Reform Party).
- Issue-based (e.g. Green Party).
- Ideological (e.g. Socialist Party, Constitution Party, Peace and Freedom Party).

Here are a few details to give you an idea of what some of these third parties stand for:

Too many candidates can name only Ross Perot or Ralph Nader. You need a wider and more typical range of examples.

- **Constitution Party:** founded as the US Taxpayers' Party in 1992 and renamed in 1999, it is a collection of formerly separate right-wing independent parties. It is strongly anti-gun control, anti-tax, anti-immigration, protectionist, anti-United Nations, anti-gay rights, pro-school prayer and pro-life.

- **Green Party:** the informal US-affiliate of the European Greens. Ideologically on the left of US politics.
- **Libertarian Party:** stands for total individual liberty. It is pro-drug legalisation, pro-choice, pro-gay marriage, pro-home schooling and anti-gun control. It also stands for total economic freedom. The 1988 Libertarian Party presidential nominee Ron Paul is now a Republican Congressman from Texas.
- **Natural Law Party:** supports transcendental meditation, yogic flying and other peaceful 'New Age' practices as remedies for the problems of US society.
- **Peace and Freedom Party:** founded in the 1960s as a left-wing party opposed to the Vietnam War. Closely associated with the 'Black Panther' movement as well as the notorious baby doctor Benjamin Spock. Has links with the Workers' World Party.

Hence the claim, often made, that there are 'no third parties' in the USA.

What the USA does not have are national, permanent third parties that regularly win at least 5% of the popular vote in general elections, like the Liberal Democrats in the UK. US third parties are either national, permanent but insignificant (such as the Libertarian Party) or they are not national and permanent. Even Ross Perot's Reform Party, after impressive nationwide performances in 1992 and 1996, disintegrated in 2000.

Candidate	Party	Popular votes	% of popular vote	Electoral College votes
Ralph Nader	Independent	463,647	0.4	0
Michael Badnarik	Libertarian	397,231	0.3	0
Michael Peroutka	Constitution	144,489	0.1	0
David Cobb	Green	119,859	0.1	0
Leonard Peltier	Peace and Freedom	27,607	0	0
Roger Calero	Socialist Workers	10,822	0	0
Thomas Harens	Christian Freedom	2,387	0	0
Bill Van Auken	Socialist Equality	1,857	0	0
John Parker	Workers World	1,646	0	0
Earl Dodge	Prohibition	140	0	0

Table 3.2 Third-party support in the 2004 presidential election

2 Recent success by third parties

In recent presidential elections, third parties have enjoyed some success, as is shown in Table 3.3.

Year	Candidate	Party	% of popular vote	Electoral College votes
1968	George Wallace	American Independent	13	46
1980	John Anderson	National Unity	7	0
1992	Ross Perot	(No party affiliation)	19	0
1996	Ross Perot	Reform	9	0

Table 3.3 Significant third-party support in presidential elections, 1968–96

Third parties have had very limited representation in Congress, as is shown in Table 3.4. They don't do much better when it comes to elections for state governors, as Table 3.5 shows.

Years	House/Senate	Name	Party	State
1971–77	Senate	James Buckley	New York Conservative	New York
1993–	House	Bernie Saunders	Socialist	Vermont
July–October 1999	Senate	Bob Smith	US Taxpayers	New Hampshire
2000–02	House	Virgil Goode	Independent	Virginia
2001–	Senate	James Jeffords	Independent	Vermont

Table 3.4 Third-party members of Congress, 1971–2005

Years	Name	Party	State
1975–79	James Longley	Independent	Maine
1991–95	Walter Hickel	Alaska Independent	Alaska
1991–95	Lowell Weicker	A Connecticut Party	Connecticut
1995–2003	Angus King	Independent	Maine
1999–2003	Jesse Ventura	Reform	Minnesota

Table 3.5 Third-party state governors, 1975–2005

3 *Difficulties facing third parties*

Third parties in the USA face a number of significant difficulties:

- **The electoral system:** the first-past the post, winner-takes-all system, which is used for every election in the USA — federal, state and local — makes life very difficult for third parties. For example, Ross Perot won 19% of the vote in 1992 but won no Electoral College votes. This is particularly true of national third parties. Regional third parties fair better. See, for example, George Wallace in 1968.
- **Federal campaign finance laws:** the way candidates can qualify for 'matching funds' puts third-party candidates at a disadvantage. Major party candidates qualify by raising at least $5,000 in contributions of $250 or less in at least 20 states. But third-party candidates qualify only by getting at least 5% of the popular vote. Not only is this a difficult hurdle, but it means that the party can qualify only in the next round of elections. Hence Ross Perot could not qualify for matching funds in 1992, but his Reform Party did qualify in 1996 and 2000 by virtue of getting more than 5% in the previous election.
- **State ballot access laws:** the way third-party candidates have to qualify to get their names on the ballot paper in each state makes life very difficult for third parties. States require third-party candidates to present a petition signed by a certain number of registered voters in the state. Whilst Tennessee requires only 25 signatures, in Montana the figure is 5% of all registered voters. This takes time and money. In 1980, John Anderson estimated that to get his name on the

Virgil Goode became a Republican in 2003.

Senator James Jeffords of Vermont switched from the Republican Party to be an Independent in May 2001.

In 1992, Ross Perot stood as a person rather than a party. He formed the Reform Party after his 1992 success. Hence one can talk of third party and 'independent' candidates to distinguish between the two.

The Reform Party did not get matching funds in 2004, having gained less than 1% of the vote in 2000.

Third parties

ballot in all 50 states, he had to collect around 1.2 million signatures nationwide and that he spent over $3 million in doing so.

- **Lack of resources:** third-party candidates are generally very short of resources — especially financial resources. They find fundraising difficult. People are reluctant to give money to parties they see as sure losers, creating something of a 'catch 22' situation.

- **Lack of media coverage:** third parties also tend to miss out on media coverage. Newspapers and television virtually ignore them. They cannot afford much if anything in the way of TV advertisements. They are generally excluded from the televised presidential debates.

- **Lack of well-known, well-qualified candidates:** again something of a self-fulfilling prophecy. Third-party candidates are unlikely to be household names and are unlikely to have held any significant political office.

- **Regarded as too ideological:** because the two major parties are so all-embracing in their ideologies, third parties are often left only the ideological fringes of the political spectrum — the Constitution Party or the Socialist Party. Others are easily linked to 'extremism' by their opponents. The following slogan, for example, was used against third-party candidate Governor George Wallace during his 1968 presidential campaign: 'If you liked Hitler, you'll love Wallace.'

- **The tactics of the two major parties:** if a third-party candidate does still manage to win significant support (e.g. Wallace in 1968, Perot in 1992), one or both of the two major parties will eventually adopt some of their policies. So, for example, Nixon pursued what he called his 'southern strategy' in 1972 to woo ex-Wallace voters. Both Governor Clinton and President Bush addressed the federal budget deficit issue in the1992 campaign after Ross Perot had got so much support by talking about it. In this sense, third parties can be seen to be the 'winners' — losing the election but winning the policy debate.

Ross Perot's inclusion in 1992 is the only exception.

Examiners sometimes hint at this when they ask questions such as 'Examine the claim that third parties always lose in presidential elections.'

Pressure groups are regarded as having important implications for a modern democracy. Through them, citizens can participate in the political process between elections. They can also use their membership of them to pressurise all three branches of government — the legislature (Congress), the executive (the president and the bureaucracy) and the judiciary, including the Supreme Court. In a country like the United States, with a participatory tradition and a more open form of government than in the UK, pressure groups seem to take on added importance. But are pressure groups always 'good' for democracy?

The topic is divided into eight major headings:

A Definition
B Types of pressure groups
C Functions of pressure groups
D Importance of pressure groups
E Pressure group activity
F Political action committees
G Influence on the federal government
H Arguments for and against pressure groups

A Definition

A pressure group is an organised interest group in which members share and actively pursue common views and objectives to influence government. Pressure groups are therefore quite distinct from political parties. Whereas political parties seek to **win control of government**, pressure groups seek to **influence** those who have won control of government.

Thus the Green Party is different from Greenpeace.

Pressure groups vary considerably in terms of size, wealth and influence. Pressure groups in the United States operate at all levels of government — federal, state and local — and seek to bring their influence to bear on all three branches of government — the legislature, the executive and the judiciary.

B Types of pressure groups

Robert McKeever has come up with a very helpful typology of interest groups and this is shown in Table 4.1.

Type	Example
Business/trade	American Business Conference
	National Association of Manufacturers
	National Automobile Dealers Association
Agriculture	American Farm Bureau Federation
	National Farmers' Union
	Associated Milk Producers Inc.

Type	Example
Unions	American Federation of Labor–Congress of Industrial Organisations (AFL–CIO) United Auto Workers
Professional	American Medical Association National Education Association American Bar Association
Single issue	Mothers Against Drunk Driving (MADD) National Rifle Association (NRA) National Abortion and Reproductive Rights Action League
Ideological	American Conservative Union People for the American Way American Civil Liberties Union (ACLU)
Group rights	National Association for the Advancement of Colored People (NAACP) National Organisation of Women (NOW) American Association of Retired Persons
Public interest	Common Cause Friends of the Earth

Table 4.1 Pressure groups: types and examples

C Functions of pressure groups

Pressure groups are said to have five basic functions:

(1) Representation — they represent the interests of various groups in society. Table 4.1 gives some examples of the types of groups that pressure groups can represent in American politics.

(2) Citizen participation — they increase the opportunities for ordinary citizens to participate in the decision-making process between elections.

(3) Public education — they attempt to educate public opinion, warning them of dangers if issues are not addressed. One can see this being done by pressure groups operating in such issue areas as the environment and gun control.

(4) Agenda building — they attempt to influence the agendas of political parties, legislators and bureaucracies to give prominence and priority to their interests. They will attempt to bring together different parts of American society — for example business groups, religious groups, state governments, professional organisations — to work together to achieve a common interest.

(5) Programme monitoring — they will scrutinise and hold government to account in the implementation of policies to try to ensure that promises are fulfilled, policies are actually 'delivered' and regulations are enforced.

D Importance of pressure groups

But why are pressure groups so important in American politics, more important than in the UK for example? Here are three important reasons for this:

Pressure groups

(1) America is a very diverse and heterogeneous society. America has been described as a 'melting pot' conveying the picture of all types of diverse groups of people mixed together. The more diverse a society is, the greater will be the variety of special interests to represent. One can see this immediately in the racial mix of American society. Another term used to refer to America is that it is the 'hyphenated society'. Everyone seems to have a prefix to their being an 'American', whether it be 'African-American', 'Cuban-American', 'Polish-American', 'Irish-American' or even 'Native-American'. And each one has its own pressure group. There are said to be almost 100 different religions that claim at least 50,000 members each. Again, here are more interests and groups to represent. And, as we saw at the beginning of Topic 1, America is a vast country spread over different regions, all with their own cultures and traditions.

(2) The American political system has a great many access points. In the UK, political power is quite highly centralised. There are few access points for the ordinary citizen to influence government. The executive branch (prime minister and cabinet) largely controls the legislature (Parliament). Parliament is made up of only one truly effective chamber (the House of Commons). The prime minister, it could be argued, exercises a good deal of relatively unchecked power. Hence there are few points at which real political decisions are made and there are therefore few access points. But in the United States there is a doctrine of 'shared powers' (see Topic 1.C) — shared between the three branches of the federal government as well as between the federal government and the state governments. Even an institution like Congress is very fragmented. It is not just on the floors of two chambers where decisions are made, but in the numerous committee rooms as well. Hence there are many points at which real political decisions are made. There are therefore many access points.

(3) The weakness of political parties in America means that citizens turn more to pressure groups. In a country such as the UK, which has strong, centralised, disciplined political parties, these parties are seen as the principal vehicles for political activity. Also in the UK, where one party will dominate the government by controlling both the executive and legislative branches of government, parties are seen as more able to deliver their promises and policy proposals. In a country such as the United States, which has relatively weak, decentralised and undisciplined political parties, parties are not seen in this light. And as we also know, these days it is highly unlikely that any one party will control (in any sense of the word) both the executive and legislative branches of the federal government. This occurred for just over 4 months between January and June 2001 (until the Republicans lost control of the Senate) and for 2 years between 1993 and 1994 when the Democrats controlled both branches. But these are the only times this has occurred since 1980.

E Pressure group activity

In recent decades, American pressure groups have been especially important in policy areas such as:

1 Environmental protection

Towards the end of the nineteenth century, as both industrialisation and 'westward expansion' were well under way, the matter of environmental conservation became important. This is when the Sierra Club was formed. This was followed in the early twentieth century by the Wilderness Society and the National Wildlife Federation. Such groups have been behind the push towards stricter laws for environmental protection.

2 Civil rights for African-Americans

The NAACP's current president, Kweisi Mfume, was a Democrat member of the House of Representatives from Maryland for 10 years before taking up this post.

The National Association for the Advancement of Colored People (NAACP) was the force behind the landmark Supreme Court decision of *Brown v. the Board of Education of Topeka* (1954) (see Topic 8.C.1) as well as the subsequent passage of much civil rights legislation. The NAACP would use its money and professional expertise to bring cases to court for people who could not otherwise afford it. These would be cases which the NAACP believed it could win and which would benefit the interests of African-Americans. The NAACP has continued to be at the centre of political debate in America over affirmative action programmes.

Affirmative action means the offering of compensatory advantages in, for example, job recruitment, to previously disadvantaged groups in society — in this case African-Americans. In the UK we tend to call it 'positive discrimination'.

3 Women's rights

Groups such as the League of Women Voters and the National Organisation of Women pushed — unsuccessfully — for the passage of an Equal Rights Amendment to the Constitution during the 1970s and 1980s. But they have remained very active in American politics, campaigning on such issues as equal pay and job opportunities for women. They have also been involved in the debate over attempting to root out sexual harassment in the workplace, with some high-profile cases in the United States military. This latter issue also received much public debate concerning President Clinton's relationships with women such as Paula Corbin Jones. Some criticised women's groups for not being more critical of the President. Women's groups have also been very much involved in the abortion debate.

4 Abortion rights

'Pro-choice' = in favour of a woman's right (to choose) to have an abortion; 'pro-life' = anti-abortion.

You will find details and other examples of presidential vetoes in Topic 6.A.4.

Both the pro-choice and pro-life lobbies have been very active in American politics during the past three to four decades. Since the 1973 *Roe v. Wade* decision by the Supreme Court (see Topic 8.C.4), pro-choice groups have fought to preserve the constitutional right of women to have an abortion, whereas the pro-life groups have fought to have it both narrowed and overturned. Most recently, they have been involved in the debate concerning the practice of so-called 'partial birth abortions'. When Congress tried to ban such types of abortion, President Clinton vetoed the bills, once in 1996 and again in 1997. In 2000, the Supreme Court refused to allow states to ban these types of abortion.

5 *Gun control*

The National Rifle Association (NRA) is arguably one of the most powerful interest groups in American politics, with a membership of some 3 million. It was formed in 1871 as a group dedicated to teaching people how to use guns. But since the 1960s, it has been very influential in stopping what it sees as encroachments on citizens' rights to own and use legal firearms. It seeks to uphold the strictest interpretation of the Second Amendment right to 'keep and bear arms'. It also works to oppose tougher gun control laws put forward at any level of government. The NRA has opposed the passage of **the Brady Bill** and the assault weapons ban, as well as laws requiring background checks on those purchasing guns and the mandatory sale of trigger locks with handguns. In the 10-year period between 1983 and 1992, the NRA spent $8 million on congressional elections. This money was spent on both supporting candidates who agreed with their position and opposing those who did not. The NRA's national president, the former Hollywood movie star Charlton Heston, has brought a huge amount of public attention to the organisation.

Named after James Brady, President Reagan's Press Secretary, who was shot and seriously wounded during the assassination attempt on the President in March 1981.

6 *Health*

Two areas where pressure groups played decisive parts during the 1990s were those of Bill Clinton's proposed health-care reforms, and proposals to limit tobacco advertising as well as legal efforts to seek compensation from tobacco companies for smokers suffering smoking-related illnesses.

F Political action committees

A political action committee (PAC) is an organisation whose purpose is to raise and then give campaign funds to candidates for political office. Because the current campaign finance laws limit the amount of money any corporation, labour union, trade association or such like can give to a candidate, PACs have evolved as a way of getting round these limitations. Although they existed before the passage of campaign finance laws in the early 1970s, their phenomenal growth occurred during the last 25 years of the twentieth century. In 1972, there were just 113 PACs in the United States. By 1982, there were 3,371 and by 1990 over 4,000. Almost half of all PACs are the creation of America's business corporations. Others have been formed by labour unions or trade and professional associations.

As with other types of pressure groups, PACs come into their own particularly at election time. It is estimated that by 2000, candidates in House races relied on PACs for 40% of their campaign money. Altogether in the 2000 election cycle, it is likely that PACs spent something in excess of a quarter of a billion dollars. Table 4.2 shows the ten largest PAC contributors to House and Senate candidates in the 1998 mid-term elections.

PAC	Contribution ($)
Realtors' Association	2,474,133
Association of Trial Lawyers	2,428,300
State, County and Municipal Employees	2,374,950
American Medical Association	2,336,281
Democratic Republican Voter Education	2,183,250
National Automobile Dealers' Association	2,107,800
United Auto Workers	1,915,460
International Brotherhood of Electrical Workers	1,884,470
National Education Association	1,853,390
National Association of Home Builders	1,807,240

Table 4.2 Top ten PAC contributors: 1998 mid-term congressional elections

Incumbent = currently in office (e.g. a sitting House or Senate member).

The other important thing to know about PACs is that they give far more money to incumbent politicians than challengers. In the 1998 election cycle, PACs gave $120 million to House incumbents but only $14 million to House challengers. It was much the same in the Senate races, where incumbents got over $30 million from PACs while challengers got only $6 million.

G Influence on the federal government

Pressure groups attempt to influence Congress, the federal bureaucracy and the courts. American government has far more 'access points' than does government in the UK. Government is thought to be more 'open'. This enhances the potential for influence by pressure groups. And in a system where political parties are clearly weaker than they are in the UK, this again increases opportunities for pressure groups to have greater degrees of influence.

1 Influence on the legislature

Also see Topic 5.G.4.

Americans do far more of this than their UK counterparts.

Pressure groups will seek to influence the way House and Senate members vote. They will do this by a number of methods, including:
- direct contact with House and Senate members and their senior staff
- direct contact with the relevant House and Senate committee members and their staff
- organising constituents to write to, phone, fax, e-mail or visit their House and Senate members to express their support for or opposition to a certain policy initiative
- publicising the voting records of House and Senate members
- endorsement of supportive members and opposition to non-supportive members in forthcoming re-election campaigns

- fundraising, campaigning for or against members of Congress — paying for radio/TV advertisements etc.

Congressional elections provide opportunities for pressure groups to play a potentially important part in the political system. Here are some examples:

- In 1996, labour unions — although usually sympathetic to Democratic candidates — backed 27 Republican House candidates who had been supportive of their interests.
- Religious groups such as the Christian Coalition will issue what they call 'voter guides', detailing candidates' positions on issues such as school prayers and abortion, to be handed out in 'sympathetic' churches just before election day.
- The Sierra Club spent over $16 million in the 1996 elections on 15 House and 8 Senate races, using advertisements that promoted some sympathetic candidates and attacked unsympathetic ones.

Pressure groups may also launch high-profile campaigns in the media when a significant piece of legislation is about to come up for a crucial debate and vote in Congress. Recent examples include congressional debates and votes on health-care reform, welfare reform, gun control and international environmental agreements.

2 Influence on the executive

Pressure groups will seek to maintain strong ties with relevant executive departments, agencies and regulatory commissions. This is especially the case when it comes to the regulatory work of the federal government — regulations, for example, regarding health and safety at work, business, the transport and communications industries, or the environment.

Problems can emerge when regulatory bodies are thought to have too cosy a relationship with the particular group they are meant to be regulating. Are they acting as 'watch dogs' or 'lap dogs'?

Edward Ashbee and Nigel Ashford (*US Politics Today*, Manchester University Press, 1999) identify another close link, that between what they call 'producer' groups — such as companies, labour unions or small business federations — and relevant government departments and agencies seeking protection, funding, subsidies or price guarantee mechanisms.

3 Influence on the judiciary

*Amicus curiae =
'Friends of the court'.*

Pressure groups can hope to influence the courts by offering *amicus curiae* briefings. Through these, pressure groups will have an opportunity to present their views to the court in writing before oral arguments are heard. Pressure groups have certainly used this to great effect in recent decades in such areas as the civil rights of racial minorities, abortion rights and First Amendment rights. They may also sponsor cases to come before the courts, as the NAACP did in the 1954 *Brown v. Board* case. They may actually bring cases themselves, such as the 1997 *Reno v. American Civil Liberties Union* case (see Topic 8.C.6).

In the last 15 years, pressure groups have also been very active in supporting or opposing the nomination of judges, especially those to the Supreme Court. They were certainly very active in the Senate confirmation hearings surrounding Robert Bork (1987) and Clarence Thomas (1991).

H Arguments for and against pressure groups

Arguments in favour of pressure groups having an important role to play in American politics stress that pressure groups provide useful functions, by acting as:

- information-givers — to members of Congress, government departments, the courts and the electorate as a whole, for whom they play an 'educating' role
- policy formulators
- a 'sounding board' for members of Congress and government departments
- enhancers of political participation, especially between elections and on specific issues

Arguments against pressure groups having as much power as they currently seem to have in American politics include the following:

Senator Edward Kennedy once commented that America has 'the finest Congress that money can buy'.

- Money becomes the all-deciding factor — you have to 'pay to play'.
- They work too much for 'special' interests and against the 'national' interests.
- They tend to be élitist and largely unaccountable, and their power thereby detracts from elected (Congress) and accountable (executive) officials.
- They lead to inequalities of power, for example in policy debates relating to health care, tobacco and gun control.
- The 'revolving door' syndrome allows former members of Congress or the executive branch to take up highly paid jobs as lobbyists: this may mean that federal officials use their position to do favours in exchange for an attractive post when they leave office.
- They sometimes use methods of 'direct action' that are deemed by others to be inappropriate, for example methods used recently by animal rights groups, pro- and anti-abortion groups, environmentalists and anti-capitalist groups.

We now move on to look at the three branches of the federal government — the legislature (Congress), the executive (the president) and the judiciary (the Supreme Court). As we saw in Topic 1, they are the branches dealt with by the first three Articles of the Constitution — Congress (Article I), the president (Article II) and the Supreme Court (Article III). Topic 5 looks at Congress, which, as the legislative branch, makes the laws. We need to know about and understand its membership, election, powers and organisation. We need to know what it does and how it does it. We also need to remember that in US politics, checks and balances are never far away. So we shall need to keep an eye out for how Congress relates to the other two branches of government.

The topic is divided into eight major headings:

A Membership and election
B Powers
C Comparison between the House and the Senate
D Leadership
E The committee system
F The legislative process
G Voting in Congress
H Reform

A Membership and election

1 Terminology

Congress is the overall name for both houses. Congress is made up of two houses — the House of Representatives and the Senate. Congress is therefore described as **bicameral** — made up of two houses or 'chambers'. There is potential confusion in the terms used to refer to members of each house. The problem lies in the fact that although the term 'Congress' refers to *both* houses, the term 'Congressman' refers only to members of the House of Representatives. Members of the Senate are called 'senators'.

> To avoid confusion, I prefer to use the term 'House members' to refer to members of the House of Representatives. One can also then use the term 'House and Senate members' to refer to both together.

2 House membership and election

In the House of Representatives there are 435 members. Each state has a certain number of members proportional to the population of the state. Except in states that have just one House member, each member represents a sub-division of the state known as a 'District'. By the time of the 2002 elections, California (the largest state) had 53, Wyoming (the smallest state) just 1. Members are elected for **2-year terms**. Elections are held on the Tuesday after the first Monday in November. In years divisible by four (e.g. 2000, 2004) these will coincide with the presidential election. Elections in the years between presidential elections (e.g. 2002, 2006) are therefore called **mid-term elections**.

> Notice the change following the 2000 census and subsequent redistribution of House seats.

The Constitution states that to be a member of the House of Representatives you must:

- be at least 25 years of age
- have been a US citizen for at least 7 years
- be a resident of the state your District is in

In the House of Representatives at the beginning of the 109th Congress (January 2005), amongst the 435 members there were:

- 64 women
- 41 African-Americans
- 23 Hispanics
- 160 lawyers
- 128 Roman Catholics
- no ex-senators

> Not a *natural-born* US citizen, as required for the presidency.

> The last ex-senator in the House was Claude Pepper of Florida, who served in the Senate 1936–50 but lost in a primary. He then served in the House from 1962 until his death in 1989.

Years	Women	African-Americans
1975–76	19	15
1977–78	18	16
1979–80	16	16
1981–82	19	17
1983–84	21	21
1985–86	22	20
1987–88	23	23
1989–90	25	24
1991–92	28	25
1993–94	47	38
1995–96	48	38
1997–98	51	38
1999–2000	56	35
2001–02	59	36
2003–04	59	38
2005–	64	41

Table 5.1 Women and African-American members of the House, 1975–2005

As Table 5.1 shows, the number of women and African-American members in the House has increased quite significantly over the past 20 years. This was particularly the case following the elections in 1992. But the 64 women members still represents only 14% of the membership, well below the percentage they make up of the US electorate. For African-Americans, the 41 members represent 9%, only slightly below their 10% in society as a whole.

> The Democrats dubbed 1992 'the year of the woman'.

Some House members will have to fight a primary — usually some time between May and September of the election year — where they will face opposition from those within their party to gain the nomination for the general election. Table 5.2 shows that very few incumbent House members are defeated in primaries or in the general election. 1992 was something of an exception to this trend.

Year	Retired	Sought re-election	Defeated in primary	Defeated in general election	Total number re-elected	% re-elected who sought re-election
1984	22	409	3	16	390	95.4
1986	38	393	2	6	385	98.0
1988	26	409	1	6	402	98.3
1990	27	407	1	15	391	96.1
1992	67	368	19	24	325	88.3
1994	48	387	4	34	349	90.2
1996	50	383	2	21	360	94.0
1998	33	401	1	6	394	98.3
2000	32	403	3	6	394	97.8
2002	38	397	8	8	381	96.0
2004	29	404	2	7	395	97.8

Table 5.2 House members: retired, defeated, re-elected, 1984–2004

3   *Senate membership and election*

In the Senate there are 100 members. Each state — regardless of population — has two senators. Each senator represents the entire state. They are elected for **6-year terms. One-third of the Senate is up for re-election every 2 years.** Senate elections are held on the same day as elections to the House.

The Constitution states that to be a senator you must:
- be at least 30 years of age
- have been a US citizen for at least 9 years
- be a resident of the state you represent

In the Senate at the beginning of the 109th Congress (January 2005), amongst the 100 members there were:
- 14 women
- 1 African-American
- 2 Hispanics
- 58 lawyers
- 24 Roman Catholics
- 52 ex-House members

Again, as in the House, the number of women members has increased of late but still stands at a proportionately low number (see Table 5.3). Following the defeat of Democrat Carol Moseley Braun of Illinois in 1998, there were no African-American senators until the election of Barack Obama in 2004. It is highly significant that over half (52) of the current Senate are former members of the House of Representatives. It is an important indicator of the perceived power and prestige of the Senate in comparison to the House.

Again, some senators may face a challenge in a primary. But, as Table 5.4 shows, it is unusual for senators to be defeated either in the primary or in the general election.

Years	Women	African-Americans
1975–76	0	1
1977–78	0	1
1979–80	1	0
1981–82	2	0
1983–84	2	0
1985–86	2	0
1987–88	2	0
1989–90	2	0
1991–92	2	0
1993–94	7	1
1995–96	8	1
1997–98	9	1
1999–2000	9	0
2001–02	13	0
2003–04	14	0
2005–	14	1

Table 5.3 Women and African-American members of the Senate, 1975–2005

Year	Retired	Sought re-election	Defeated in primary	Defeated in general election	Total number re-elected	% re-elected who sought re-election
1984	4	29	0	3	26	89.6
1986	6	28	0	7	21	75.0
1988	6	27	0	4	23	85.2
1990	3	32	0	1	31	96.9
1992	7	28	1	4	23	82.1
1994	9	26	0	2	24	92.3
1996	13	21	1	1	19	90.5
1998	5	29	0	3	26	89.6
2000	5	29	0	5	24	82.8
2002	5	28	1	3	24	85.7
2004	8	26	0	1	25	96.1

Table 5.4 Senators: retired, defeated, re-elected, 1984–2004

B Powers

In terms of powers, each house has **exclusive powers** and **joint powers**. In other words, each house has powers that they alone — and not the other house — possess. Equally, each house shares powers with the other house.

1 *Exclusive powers*

The House of Representatives has three exclusive powers:
(1) To begin consideration of all money bills.
(2) To impeach any member of the executive or judicial branches of the federal government.
(3) To elect the president if the Electoral College is deadlocked.

The Founding Fathers gave the House of Representatives **the power to begin consideration of all money bills** because it was the only directly elected chamber at that time.

Impeachment means 'making a formal accusation' or 'bringing charges' against any member of the other two branches. We saw this in 1998 when the House of Representatives impeached President Clinton on two counts — perjury and obstruction of justice. President Clinton was the seventeenth person to be impeached by the House since the first case in 1797, but only the second president. President Andrew Johnson was impeached — and acquitted by the Senate — in 1868. Other than two presidents, those impeached have included:

- 1 senator
- 1 Supreme Court justice
- 2 Cabinet members
- 11 District (trial court) judges

The third power — **to elect the president if the Electoral College is deadlocked** — is now almost redundant, not having been used since 1824.

The Senate has four exclusive powers:
(1) To ratify all treaties negotiated by the president — **a two-thirds majority required**.
(2) To confirm many appointments (to the executive and judicial branches) made by the president — **a simple majority required**.
(3) To try cases of impeachment — **a two-thirds majority required** to convict.
(4) To elect the vice-president if the Electoral College is deadlocked.

It is the first two of these exclusive powers that go some way to making the Senate the more powerful and prestigious of the two chambers.

Only the Senate has the power to **ratify treaties and confirm appointments**. Although the Senate usually agrees, remember that presidents will generally only submit those treaties and appointments that they know the Senate will approve. Thus the Senate has a kind of hidden power. In 1999, the Senate rejected the Comprehensive Test Ban Treaty. The vote was 48–51, 18 votes short of the two-thirds majority required. The same year, the Senate rejected President Clinton's nomination of Ronnie White to be a judge on the federal trial court. The vote here was 45–54, 5 votes short of the simple majority required.

Once the House has impeached someone, the Senate **tries that case of impeachment**. To find that person guilty, two-thirds of the senators voting must vote 'guilty'. In the votes on the two charges brought against President Clinton,

The term 'impeachment' is often misunderstood. It simply means to make a formal accusation against someone.

Senator William Blount was accused in 1797 of 'aiding the British'! Supreme Court Justice Samuel Chase was accused in 1804 of making 'harsh, partisan and unfair' decisions.

the Senate voted 45–55 and 50–50, respectively 22 and 17 votes short of the two-thirds majority required. The last person to be found guilty by the Senate — and thus removed from office — was District Court Judge Walter Nixon. He was impeached and found guilty of perjury in 1989.

The final exclusive Senate power — **to elect the vice-president if the Electoral College is deadlocked** — remains unused since 1824.

2 Joint powers

Together, the House of Representatives and the Senate have five joint powers:
(1) To pass legislation, including the budget.
(2) To conduct investigations regarding the actions of the executive branch.
(3) To initiate constitutional amendments.
(4) To declare war.
(5) To confirm the appointment of a newly appointed vice-president.

It is very important to remember that the House and the Senate share arguably the most important power of Congress, that of **passing legislation**. Unlike in the UK Parliament, where the House of Commons dominates the legislative process, in the US Congress the two chambers have equal legislative power. This can be seen in the following ways:
- All legislation must pass through all stages in **both houses**.
- **Both houses** conduct detailed scrutiny of legislation in committee.
- **Both houses** have full power of amendment over all bills, usually resulting in there being two different versions of the same bill once it has gone through both houses.
- Conference committees — set up to reconcile the two different versions of the same bill — are made up of members of **both houses** and their decisions must be agreed to by **both houses**.
- It takes a two-thirds majority in **both houses** to override a presidential veto.

Both houses have standing committees, which can conduct investigations of the work of the executive branch. Both houses can also establish select committees to perform the same function.

In order **to propose an amendment to the Constitution**, a two-thirds majority is required in both houses (see Topic 1.B.4).

The joint power **to declare war** has become somewhat redundant. The power has not been used since December 1941, when Congress declared war on Japan following the attack on Pearl Harbor. That was the fifth time it had been used, the others being:
- the war of 1812
- the Mexican war in 1848
- the Spanish–American war in 1898
- the First World War in 1917

The final joint power is relatively new, having been granted in 1967 by the 25th Amendment. Should the office of the vice-presidency become vacant

Notice that they confirm only a newly *appointed* vice-president, not one who is elected.

This was against Great Britain.

between elections, the president is now empowered to nominate a new vice-president to fill the vacancy. But the nomination must be confirmed by a simple majority vote in both houses of Congress. The power has been used twice — in 1973 and 1974. In 1973, Vice-President Spiro Agnew resigned after pleading 'no contest' to a charge of income tax evasion. President Nixon appointed the Republican (Minority) Leader of the House of Representatives Gerald Ford as his new vice-president. Ford was confirmed by the Senate by 92 votes to 3, and by the House 387–35.

This related to matters when Agnew was Governor of Maryland.

Less than a year later, President Nixon resigned and Ford became president, again leaving the vice-presidency vacant. Ford chose former New York Governor Nelson Rockefeller. Rockefeller was easily confirmed in the Senate (90–7) but found things tougher in the House (287–128).

C Comparison between the House and the Senate

Having looked at the membership and powers of both houses, let us compare the two houses. It is often suggested that the Senate is more powerful and prestigious than the House. Is this the case? There is a 'yes' and a 'no' answer. Let us consider each in turn.

This has been a frequent focus for A-level questions. Too many candidates forget to argue the 'no' side.

Reasons why the Senate is often thought of as being more prestigious and powerful than the House of Representatives are:

- Senators **represent the entire state**, not just part of the state.
- Senators **serve 6-year terms**, three times as long as House members.
- As a Senator you are **one of 100**, rather than one of 435, as is the case for House members.
- Senators are therefore **likely to chair a committee** much sooner in their career than their House counterparts.
- Senators often enjoy much **greater name recognition**, not only in their state but often across the nation as a whole.
- **House members frequently seek election to the Senate**; the reverse is almost unknown.
- Senators are more frequently **thought of as likely presidential candidates**. Recent examples include Senators John Kerry and John Edwards (2004).
- Senators are **more frequently nominated as vice-presidential running-mates**. Recent examples include Senators Dan Quayle (1988), Al Gore (1992), Joseph Lieberman (2000) and John Edwards (2004).
- Senators have **exclusive powers**, including the ratification of treaties and the confirmation of appointments, which are generally agreed to be more significant than the exclusive powers enjoyed by House members.

Currently there are 52 ex-House members in the Senate but no ex-Senators in the House.

	Senate	House
Number of members	100	435
Number per state	2	Proportional to population
Length of term	6 years	2 years
Age qualification	30	25
Citizenship qualification	9 years	7 years
Average age	60	55
Presiding officer	Vice-president	Speaker
Number of women	14	64
Number of African-Americans	1	41
Ex-members of other house	52	0
Special powers	(i) Ratify treaties (ii) Confirm appointments (iii) Try cases of impeachment (iv) Elect vice-president if Electoral College is deadlocked	(i) Initiate money bills (ii) Impeachment (iii) Elect president if Electoral College is deadlocked
Joint powers	(i) Legislation (ii) Declare war (iii) Initiate constitutional amendments (iv) Confirm newly appointed vice-president	

Table 5.5 Senate and House compared

However, it is also important to remember that in some ways Senate and House members are equal. The most important argument here concerns the equality of the two houses in the legislative process:

- All bills must go through all stages **in both houses**; neither can overturn the decisions of the other.
- **Both houses** have powerful standing committees, which conduct separate hearings at the all-important committee stage.
- At the conference committee stage, **members of both houses** are represented.
- **Both houses** must agree to the compromise reached at the conference committee.
- To override a presidential veto, a two-thirds majority in **both houses** is required.

D Leadership

The main leadership posts in Congress are:

- the Speaker of the House of Representatives
- the Majority and Minority Leaders of both houses
- standing committee chairs

1 Speaker of the House of Representatives

Currently Dennis Hastert, a Republican, from Illinois, first elected as Speaker in 1999.

The Speaker of the House of Representatives is:
- elected by the entire House membership at the beginning of each new Congress (i.e. every 2 years)
- usually the nominee of the majority party in the House at the time
- not required by the Constitution to be a serving member of the House, though all Speakers have been
- next in line to the presidency after the vice-president, but this is less significant with the passage of the 25th Amendment requiring the vice-presidency to be filled if a vacancy should occur there

Unlike the Speaker of the House of Commons, the Speaker of the House of Representatives is a political player, not just a neutral umpire. In essence, the Speaker is the leader of the majority party in the House and, if of a different party from the president, may act as the major spokesperson for the party, a kind of 'leader of the opposition'.

That is, chairs debates.

The Speaker has the following powers and functions:
- Acts as the presiding officer of the House.
- Interprets and enforces the rules of the House, decides points of order.
- Refers bills to committees.
- Appoints select and conference committee chairs.
- Appoints majority party members of the House Rules Committee.
- May exercise considerable influence in the flow of legislation through the House, as well as in committee assignments for majority party members and even the selection of House standing committee chairs.

This was certainly true of Newt Gingrich (Speaker 1995–98).

Some Speakers have become politicians of considerable stature and importance. Recent examples would include Democrat Tip O'Neill and Republican Newt Gingrich. Others such as Dennis Hastert are more low-key.

2 Majority and Minority Leaders

In both the House and the Senate, there is a Majority and Minority Leader. They are elected by their respective party groups in each house every 2 years at the start of each Congress.

In both houses, the Majority and Minority Leaders:
- act as day-by-day 'directors of operations' on the floor of their respective houses
- hold press briefings to talk about their party's policy agenda
- act as liaison between the House/Senate and the White House
- in the Senate, make **unanimous consent agreements** to bring bills for debate on the Senate floor (see F.3)

In the House, the Majority Leader plays a 'number two' role to the Speaker. The Majority and Minority Leaders may hope to become Speaker. Most Speakers — though not Dennis Hastert — previously held one of these two posts.

E The committee system

There are many different types of committee in both houses of Congress. The most important are:

- standing committees
- the House Rules Committee
- conference committees
- select committees

1 *Standing committees*

1.1 Membership

House standing committee	Chair
Agriculture	Bob Goodlatte of Virginia
Appropriations	Jerry Lewis of California
Armed Services	Duncan Hunter of California
Budget	Jim Nussle of Iowa
Education and the Workforce	John Boehner of Ohio
Energy and Commerce	Joe Barton of Texas
Financial Services	Michael Oxley of Ohio
Government Reform	Tom Davis of Virginia
International Relations	Henry Hyde of Illinois
Judiciary	James Sensenbrenner of Wisconsin
Resources	Richard Pombo of California
Rules	David Dreier of California
Science	Sherwood Boehlert of New York
Small Business	Donald Manzullo of Illinois
Standards of Official Conduct	Doc Hastings of Washington
Transportation and Infrastructure	Don Young of Alaska
Veterans' Affairs	Steve Buyer of Indiana
Ways and Means	Bill Thomas of California

Table 5.6 House standing committee chairs, 2005

'Standing' = permanent.

Standing committees exist in both houses of Congress. They are **permanent, policy specialist committees**. There are 16 in each house. In the House there are also two rather different standing committees — the House Rules Committee, which timetables bills on the House floor (see E.2), and the Standards of Official Conduct Committee, which deals with the professional and ethical conduct of House members. Most standing committees are divided into subcommittees. So, for example, one of the subcommittees of the House Agriculture Committee is the Livestock and Horticulture Subcommittee, whilst the subcommittees of the Senate Armed Services Committee include one on Seapower and another on Strategic Forces.

A typical Senate standing committee has around 18 members on it, whilst a typical House standing committee is made up of around 45–50 members.

The party balance in each standing committee is in the same proportion to that which exists within the chamber as a whole. In the House of Representatives at the beginning of the 109th Congress (January 2005), the Republicans had a 232–202 advantage over Democrats, with 1 Independent. So the 46-member House Agriculture Committee had a 25–21 Republican–Democrat balance. In the Senate, the party split was 55–44, with 1 Independent. So the 24-member Senate Armed Services Committee had a 13–11 split between Republicans and Democrats.

But with Republican chairs.

Standing committee chairs are always drawn from the majority party in that particular house. Thus in January 2005, all House and Senate standing committee chairs were Republicans. The **seniority rule** states that the chair of a standing committee will be the member of the majority party with **the longest continuous service on that committee**. Referred to by its critics as the 'senility rule', it has now been relaxed, especially in the House of Representatives. Also in the House, the Republicans imposed 6-year limits on the tenure of all standing committee chairs from January 1995. This resulted in 14 House standing committees having a new chair in January 2001.

Make sure you get that right.

Senate standing committee	Chair
Agriculture, Nutrition and Forestry	Saxby Chambliss of Georgia
Appropriations	Thad Cochran of Mississippi
Armed Services	John Warner of Virginia
Banking, Housing and Urban Affairs	Richard Shelby of Alabama
Budget	Judd Gregg of New Hampshire
Commerce, Science and Transportation	Ted Stevens of Alaska
Energy and Natural Resources	Pete Domenici of New Mexico
Environment and Public Works	James Inhofe of Oklahoma
Finance	Charles Grassley of Iowa
Foreign Relations	Richard Lugar of Indiana
Governmental Affairs and Homeland Security	Susan Collins of Maine
Health, Education, Labor and Pensions	Mike Enzi of Wyoming
Judiciary	Arlen Specter of Pennsylvania
Rules and Administration	Trent Lott of Mississippi
Small Business	Olympia Snowe of Maine
Veterans' Affairs	Larry Craig of Idaho

Table 5.7 Senate standing committee chairs, 2005

1.2 Functions

House standing committees have two functions. Senate standing committees have the same two plus another. These functions are:

(1) To conduct the committee stage of the legislative process.

(2) To conduct investigations within the committee's policy area.

(3) **(In the Senate only)** To begin the confirmation process of numerous presidential appointments to both the executive and judicial branches of the federal government.

To fulfil these functions, standing committees hold **hearings** attended by **witnesses**. At the conclusion of hearings — which may last anything from a few hours to a day, to a week, or a month or more — votes will be taken to recommend action to the full chamber.

2 House Rules Committee

Officially this is one of the standing committees of the House, but it performs such a different function that it is better dealt with separately.

Nearly all bills pass through the House Rules Committee. It has the following functions:

- Timetables bills for consideration on the floor of the House.
- Deals with getting bills from the committee stage to the second reading.
- Prioritises the most important bills, giving them quick passage to the House floor.
- Gives a 'Rule' to each bill passing on to the floor for its second reading —the 'Rule' sets out the rules of debate by stating, for example, what, if any, amendments can be made to the bill at this stage.

> A 'Rule' is best thought of as a kind of admission ticket to the House floor.

For these reasons, the House Rules Committee is potentially a very important committee.

3 Conference committees

Conference committees are required because of two important characteristics about the legislative process in the US Congress. First, both houses have equal power. Second, bills pass through both houses concurrently. As a consequence, there are two different versions of each bill — a House version and a Senate version. And by the time the bill has passed through each house, the two versions are likely to be very different. If after the third reading in each house the two versions of the bill are different, and if these differences cannot be sorted out informally, then a conference committee is set up.

> In the UK Parliament, bills pass through one house and then the other, not both at the same time.

Conference committees (whose members are referred to as 'conferees'):

- are ad hoc — set up to consider a particular bill and then disbanded
- contain members of both houses
- have one function — **to reconcile the differences between the two versions of the same bill**

> 'Ad hoc' = temporary.

When the conference committee has come up with an agreed version of the bill, this must be agreed to by a vote on the floor of each house.

4 ## *Select committees*

Select committees are sometimes known as 'special committees' or 'investigative committees'. Nearly all are ad hoc, set up specially to investigate something in particular. Why have these select committees when, as we have already seen, the standing committees have an investigative function?

A select committee will be set up when the investigation either:
- does not fall within the policy area of one standing committee; or
- is likely to be so time-consuming that a standing committee would become tied up with it, thus preventing the standing committee from fulfilling its other functions.

Some examples of high-profile select committees from recent decades include:
- the Senate Select Committee on the Central Intelligence Agency
- the House Select Committee on political assassinations
- the Joint Select Committee on the Iran-Contra affair
- the Senate Select Committee on the Whitewater affair

F # The legislative process

The legislative process in the US Congress is best thought of in seven stages:
(1) First reading
(2) Committee stage
(3) Timetabling
(4) Second reading
(5) Third reading
(6) Conference committee
(7) Presidential action

It is also important to remember the following points:
- **Both houses have equal power** when dealing with legislation.
- **Bills pass through the House and Senate concurrently**.
- A 'Congress' lasts for 2 years.
- Any bills not completed in one Congress must start the process again at the beginning in the next Congress.
- A huge number of bills — around 9,000 — are introduced during a Congress.
- Only a small proportion of these — around 400 — will be successfully passed into law.
- The process is difficult and complicated.
- Supporters of a bill must win at every stage, whilst opponents have only to win at one stage to defeat a bill.
- There is little in the way of party discipline in Congress, which increases the difficulties.

But in reality there is about 20 months between one set of congressional elections and another to get bills through the process.

The legislative process

- The president is unlikely to have his own party in control of both houses of Congress.
- It is even possible that the House and the Senate may be controlled by different parties, as between June 2001 and December 2002, with the Democrats controlling the Senate and the Republicans controlling the House.

Table 5.8 gives you some idea as to the workload of recent Congresses. It is most important to note how few of the bills introduced are actually enacted.

	106th Congress 1999–2000	107th Congress 2001–02	108th Congress 2003–04
Bills introduced	10,840	8,948	10,669
Laws enacted	580 (5%)	377 (4%)	498 (5%)

Table 5.8 Workload of Congress, 1999–2004

1 First reading

- All 'money bills' must be introduced into the House first.
- There is no debate and no vote.
- It is just a formality.
- In the House, bills are placed in a hopper on the clerk's desk.
- In the Senate, the title is read out.
- Bills are then immediately sent on to the committee stage.

2 Committee stage

In the UK Parliament, the committee stage comes *after* the second reading.

- Bills are referred to one of the permanent, policy specialist standing committees (see E.1).
- It is important to note that the **committee stage comes before the second reading**.
- Committees have full power of amendment.
- Because of huge numbers of bills being referred to each committee, many bills are **pigeon-holed** — that is, merely put to one side and never considered.
- For a bill that is to be considered, a **hearing** is held with **witnesses** appearing before the committee.
- Hearings may be conducted either in the full committee or in **sub-committee**.
- Hearings can last from hours to days, weeks or even months, depending on the length of the bill and whether or not it is controversial.
- Once the hearings have been completed, the committee holds a **mark-up** session — making the changes it wishes — before **reporting out** the bill, effectively sending it on to its next stage.

The committee stage of a bill is of the utmost importance because:
- the committee members are regarded as the policy specialists so others look to the committee for a lead
- it is as far as most bills get
- committees have full power of amendment
- committees really do have life-and-death power over bills

Most textbooks do not give this as a separate stage, but I think it helps to make things clearer.

3 | *Timetabling*

By the time Congress has been in session for a few months, a huge number of bills will be waiting to come to the floor of the House and the Senate for their second reading. Whilst there are dozens of committee and subcommittee rooms in each house, there is only one floor in each chamber. There develops something of a legislative traffic jam, with bills queuing for their turn on the House and Senate floors. Each house has a procedure for dealing with this potential problem.

The House of Representatives deals with this through the **House Rules Committee** (see E.2). The Senate deals with it through what are called **unanimous consent agreements**. These, in effect, are agreements between the Senate Majority and Minority Leaders (see D.2) on the order in which bills will be debated on the Senate floor.

A filibuster is the right of continuous debate. It can be ended by a 'closure' (or 'cloture') motion, which must be approved by three-fifths of the entire Senate (i.e. 60).

A recorded vote is sometimes called a 'roll-call vote'. In the Senate the clerk still 'calls the roll' of the 100 names alphabetically. In the House it is now a vote 'by electronic device'. Fifteen minutes is usually allowed for members to cast their votes.

4 | *Second reading*

- The first opportunity for most members to debate the bill.
- In the House, most bills are debated in the **Committee of the Whole House**, allowing for different rules of debate.
- In the Senate, bills can be subject to **filibustering**.
- In both houses, further amendments can usually be made.
- Votes will be taken on amendments — simple majorities required to pass.
- At the end of the debate, a vote will be taken on the bill.
- The vote will be either a **voice vote** (for non-controversial bills) or a **recorded vote**, in which a record of each member's vote is made.
- A simple majority is required to pass the bill.

5 | *Third reading*

- A final opportunity to debate the bill.
- If substantial amendments were made at the second reading, the third reading is likely to occur some weeks or months after the second reading and require another substantive debate.
- If few amendments were made at the second reading, or these amendments were approved by large majorities, the third reading may follow on almost immediately after the second reading and be a very brief debate.
- At the end of the debate, another vote will be taken.

6 | *Conference committee*

Members are called 'conferees'.

- An optional stage.
- Members are drawn from both houses.
- If the House version and the Senate version of the bill are the same, there is no need for a conference committee.

- If differences in the two versions of the bill can be sorted out amicably between the two houses, there is no need for a conference committee.
- If there are **substantial differences** between the two versions of the bill and these **cannot be sorted out amicably**, then a conference committee will be required (see E.3).

7 *Presidential action*

A bill can be passed to the president once the House and Senate have agreed on a single version of the bill.

The president always has **three options**:
(1) To sign the bill into law: this he will do to bills he fully supports, wants to be associated with and take credit for; he must sign the bill within ten congressional workings days of receiving it.

(2) To leave the bill on his desk: this he will do to bills he only partly supports, those he takes no position on at all, or those he would wish to veto but has decided not to. These bills will become law without his signature within ten congressional working days.

(3) To veto the bill: this he will do to bills he clearly opposes. He must veto the bill within ten congressional working days of receiving it by sending it back to its house of origin with a note explaining his objections. To override the veto, the bill must be passed by a **two-thirds majority in both houses**. This is very difficult to achieve. Congress managed to override only two of Bill Clinton's 36 regular vetoes in 8 years. In 1995, they overrode his veto of the Securities Bill, which would have limited lawsuits by the shareholders of companies. In 1997, they overrode his veto of a defence spending bill. (For more detail on presidential vetoes, see Topic 6.A.4.)

At the end of a congressional session, the president has a **fourth option**:
(4) To pocket-veto the bill: if, whilst the bill is awaiting the president's action, the congressional session ends, the bill is lost. This is called a **pocket veto** and it cannot be overridden by Congress.

For about a year during the Clinton presidency, the president had a **fifth option** — **the line-item veto**. This allowed him to sign parts of a bill into law whilst vetoing other parts to do with spending. But in 1998, the Supreme Court declared the power unconstitutional.

President George W. Bush used no vetoes during his first term.

President Clinton used only one pocket veto during his entire 8 years, when he pocket-vetoed a consumer bankruptcy reform bill in December 2000.

During the brief time that President Clinton had the power, he used it on 11 bills.

G Voting in Congress

In 2004, senators cast 216 votes and House members 544.

House and Senate members are called upon to cast a large number of votes each year. They might be voting on budgets, amendments to bills, second or third readings, bills from conference committees, constitutional amendments, or in the Senate on treaties or appointments made by the president. And they will probably be rushing to the floor to cast their vote, having just broken off a committee hearing or a meeting with constituents or staff.

What factors make them vote as they do? In the UK House of Commons, the answer would be quite simple — party. But in the US Congress, political parties are only one of a number of factors that determine the way members vote.

One should consider six important determinants of voting:
(1) Political party
(2) Constituents
(3) The administration
(4) Pressure groups
(5) Colleagues and staff
(6) Personal beliefs

The relative importance of these determinants will vary from one politician to another and from one vote to another.

1 *Political party*

Political party is one of a number of determinants of voting in Congress. For some members, on some issues, it may be the most important determinant. But it is by no means the all-important determinant that it is for MPs in the UK House of Commons.

There are five important reasons for this difference:
(1) Political parties in the US are far less centralised and ideologically cohesive than their UK counterparts.
(2) US political parties do not have the 'sticks' and 'carrots' that their UK counterparts have as incentives to party unity — 'sticks' such as threats of de-selection or 'carrots' such as much sought-after jobs in the executive branch.
(3) Constituents control the selection of candidates — through congressional primaries — so House and Senate members have to be far more watchful of constituents' views than of the party view.
(4) House members are subject to elections every 2 years, increasing their reliance on the views of their constituents.
(5) The executive branch does not depend for its existence on getting its policies through the legislature, as it does in the UK.

It is also important to realise what political commentators mean in the US by a **party vote** in the legislature. In the UK House of Commons, a party vote would mean all the MPs on the government side of the House voting against all the MPs on the opposition side. A huge number of votes in the UK House of Commons would fit that description. But in the US Congress, when we talk of a party vote we mean one in which the majority of one party votes against the majority of the other party.

Take the example of a vote in the House of Representatives, on the 9/11 Recommendations Implementation bill on 8 October 2004:
● It passed by 282 to 134.
● Republicans voted 213 yes; 8 no.
● Democrats voted 69 yes; 125 no.
● The Independent House member voted 'no'.

- The majority of Republicans voted 'yes'.
- The majority of Democrats voted 'no'.

Therefore this would classify as a 'party vote', despite the fact that 77 members (8 Republicans and 69 Democrats) broke with their party majorities.

Despite this very low threshold for qualifying as a 'party vote', in recent years only around 50–60% of votes in each chamber have been party votes, as Table 5.9 shows.

Year	House	Senate
1994	62%	52%
1995	73%	69%
1996	56%	62%
1997	50%	50%
1998	56%	56%
1999	47%	63%
2000	43%	49%
2001	55%	40%
2002	43%	45%
2003	52%	67%
2004	47%	52%

Table 5.9 Party votes as a percentage of all recorded votes, 1994–2004

A more typical vote in the House or the Senate is one in which the majority of members of both parties vote the same way.

Take, for example, a vote in the House, on 7 December 2004, on the Intelligence Reform and Terrorism Prevention bill:

- It passed by 336–75.
- Republicans voted 152–67.
- Democrats voted 183–8.
- Independent voted 1–0.

2 Constituents

Why do House and Senate members place the views of their constituents so highly in their voting priorities?

There are four reasons to consider:

(1) The Constitution states that House and Senate members must be residents of the state they represent, so this gives them a good understanding of what 'the folks back home' are saying.

This is known as the 'locality rule'.

(2) A number of states go further by insisting that House members reside in the actual district (constituency) they represent.

(3) Many House and Senate members will have been born and educated, lived and worked in the state/district they now represent.

(4) House members are especially careful about constituents' views because they have to face election every 2 years.

How do House and Senate members find out what their constituents want whilst they are working in Washington DC? There are various methods, which include:

- visits from constituents
- phone calls, letters, faxes and e-mails from constituents
- keeping in constant touch with their offices back in the state/district
- reading the newspapers published in their state/district

But they will also discover what their constituents want by making frequent visits back to their state/district. The frequency will depend on how far this is from Washington DC. Once back in their state/district, House and Senate members will:

- hold party meetings
- hold 'town hall' meetings
- conduct 'surgeries' with individual constituents
- make visits around the state/district
- appear on local radio phone-in programmes
- be interviewed by representatives of the local media
- address various groups such as chambers of commerce, professional groups, Round Table lunches etc.
- visit local schools, hospitals and businesses

All these will help them keep in touch with the views of their constituents.

This is very important. Candidates too often talk of constituency interest as if on all issues everyone in the state or district thinks the same way. Would that it were that simple!

However, when it comes to voting, three further factors must be remembered:

(1) Except on some exceptional issues, local opinion on any given issue is likely to be divided with some in favour and some against.

(2) Through constituency mail and visits, the House/Senate member is more likely to hear from the discontented than the content.

(3) A member of Congress is meant to be more than just a mere 'delegate' of their constituents and may need to balance other factors, as well as the national good, against what is perceived as being merely locally popular.

3 *The administration*

The term 'administration' means members of the executive branch. Remember that much of the legislation being voted on in Congress will have been initiated by the president or members of his administration. Cabinet members — the heads of the 14 executive departments — will have a keen interest in the passage of legislation affecting their policy areas. So members of the administration — from the departments and agencies as well as the White House itself — will keep in contact with members of Congress and will attempt to persuade them to cast their votes in certain ways. They will do this through phone calls as well as visits. They will talk with members of the relevant committees, with staff members working in the Washington offices of House and Senate members.

Often, the White House itself will get involved. This will be done either by the Congressional Liaison Office or directly by the president himself.

Such persuasion will need to be regular and bipartisan. It is important that members of Congress are approached not only just before an important vote

G *Voting in Congress*

is coming up. It is also important that those from departments and the White House are willing to do favours in return, offering a two-way street of mutual cooperation. And all this will need to be done with members from both parties. For an administration to talk only with members of their party is usually a recipe for disaster. Things tend to happen in Congress when they are supported by a bipartisan coalition.

'Bipartisan' = of two parties.

4 Pressure groups

Pressure groups will use a number of different ways to try to influence the way House and Senate members cast their votes. These include contacts with members and staff in Congress, as well as attempts to generate public support favourable to their position. They will make visits and phone calls, provide evidence to support their position, organise rallies, demonstrations and petition drives both in Washington and around the country, as well as engage in significant fundraising. Money raised will be used to fund politicians who support their cause and to seek to defeat those who do not. Certain policy areas have seen significant pressure group activity, including the environment, abortion, gun control, health care, welfare reform and international trade (see Topic 4).

5 Colleagues and staff

Remember that members of Congress have to cast literally hundreds of votes every year. No politician can know all the details of all these votes. They will therefore tend to rely on other people for help in how they might vote.

Before going to the floor to vote, many House and Senate members will have checked with:

Don't underestimate the importance of senior staff. I have been with a House member walking to the House to vote, who turned to a staff member and said: 'How am I voting on this one?'

- their senior legislative staff
- fellow members of their own party who share their philosophy and views, especially senior, respected members who may become almost their mentors
- members from the same state and, in the House, members from neighbouring districts
- members of the relevant standing committee who considered the legislation at the committee stage

6 Personal beliefs

On certain votes, a House or Senate member may vote in a certain way because of their own personal beliefs. Issues upon which this factor is likely to be uppermost will be votes regarding such matters as abortion, capital punishment, tax increases (or tax cuts), federal subsidies or defence spending. There are, for example, members of Congress who because of their own personal beliefs will never vote for federal subsidies to any industry or group, even if that means going against a party line, the administration's views or their own constituents.

H Reform

Congress began to reform itself back in the 1970s. This was largely brought about by a huge influx of new members — mainly in the House of Representatives — following the mid-term elections of 1974. These elections were held just 3 months after President Nixon was forced to resign over Watergate. Into the House came a large number of newly elected, young, generally liberal Democrats, many from the big cities in the Northeast. They found a Congress dominated by long-serving, old, generally conservative Democrats, mainly from the South. They focused their reform on the standing committees of Congress.

The 1970s reforms meant that in the House standing committees:
- committee chairs are now elected by secret ballot
- committees can now be called into session by a majority vote of their members
- no member is able to chair more than one committee
- committees with 20+ members have at least four subcommittees
- subcommittees choose their own chairs, have their own budgets and hire their own staff
- committee hearings are held in public unless members vote for a 'closed' hearing

Professor Anthony King has said that as a result of these reforms, 'the powerful few have become the considerably less powerful many'.

All these reforms substantially reduced the power of the House standing committee chairs, who had previously run their own committees and subcommittees like a private fiefdom. Similar, though rather less dramatic, reforms were made in the Senate.

In 1974, there was also a substantial reform of the budget process, the setting-up of new Budget Committees in both the House and the Senate and of the Congressional Budget Office.

But the public esteem in which Congress was held declined steadily through the 1980s. By 1992, a CBS/*New York Times* poll showed that 71% of Americans disapproved of the way Congress was doing its job. Fuelled by numerous scandals and a hefty rise in congressional salaries, the voters took their revenge in the 1994 mid-term elections. Thirty-eight House Democrats and two Senate Democrats were defeated and the Democratic Party lost control of both houses of Congress for the first time since 1954!

This resulted in 14 new standing committee chairs in the House in 2001.

This brought about a further raft of congressional reforms in 1995, this time enacted by the new Republican members. Included in the 1995 reforms were:
- a cut in the number of congressional committees — from 252 to 198 — including a reduction in House standing committees from 22 to 19 and in their subcommittees from 115 to 84
- term limits for House standing committee chairs — a new limit of three terms
- term limits for the House Speaker — a new limit of four terms
- an almost total ban on House and Senate members' receipt of gifts
- a ban on House and Senate members receiving speaking fees ('honoraria')
- a significant cut in use of free mailing ('the frank')

- a requirement that Congress comply with numerous federal laws from which it had previously exempted itself, such as the Civil Rights Act, the Equal Pay Act, the Family and Medical Care Leave Act

A reform which many Americans seemed to want to impose on Congress was a limit on congressional terms of office. The Term Limits movement wanted to do to Congress what had been done to the President back in 1951 with the 22nd Amendment. The most popular proposal was to limit House members to six 2-year terms and senators to two 6-year terms. But after gaining considerable support in the early 1990s, support waned following the 1994 mid-term elections. The term limit opponents' argument that Americans already had term limits — 'they are called elections' — seemed to be somewhat proved when many senior members of both houses were swept away that November.

There are two popular misconceptions about the US presidency. The first is that it is purely a **one-man band**. Although 'the president' might be thought of as such, 'the presidency' is much more like an **orchestra**, and a large one at that, made up of literally hundreds of people. The second misconception is that the president is **hugely powerful** — 'the most powerful person in the world' is a much-used phrase. Again, although there may be a grain of truth in this, students of US politics need to discover that the office of the US president is often **very limited** and, for its occupant, hugely frustrating. The presidency is therefore something of a paradox.

Note that a president's term of office begins the year after the election. The election is in November, but the new president does not take over until the following January.

President	Party	Dates
John Kennedy	Democrat	1961–63
Lyndon Johnson	Democrat	1963–69
Richard Nixon	Republican	1969–74
Gerald Ford	Republican	1974–77
Jimmy Carter	Democrat	1977–81
Ronald Reagan	Republican	1981–89
George Bush	Republican	1989–93
Bill Clinton	Democrat	1993–2001
George W. Bush	Republican	2001–

Table 6.1 American presidents since 1961

The topic is divided into six major headings:

A The powers of the president
B The federal bureaucracy
C The cabinet
D The Executive Office of the President
E Relations with Congress
F Limits on presidential power

A The powers of the president

The powers of the president are his tasks, functions or duties. They are laid out in Article II of the Constitution. Essentially, they are the same for every president. These powers have been held by George Washington and George W. Bush, and all the 41 presidents in between.

The president has the following powers:
- To propose legislation to Congress.
- To submit the annual budget to Congress.
- To sign legislation passed by Congress.
- To veto legislation passed by Congress.
- To act as chief executive.

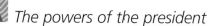

[handwritten margin notes: "appoint c minister", "patronage", "declare war"]

- To nominate executive branch officials.
- To nominate judges.
- To act as commander-in-chief.
- To negotiate treaties.
- To pardon felons.

1 Propose legislation

The phrase comes from Article II, Section 3: 'He shall from time to time give to the Congress information of the state of the Union.'

The president proposes legislation to Congress in a number of ways — most obviously through the annual **State of the Union Address**, when he addresses a joint session of Congress. This occurs each January, and it gives the president the chance to set out a legislative agenda for the coming year. But the president can propose legislation at any time by, for example, calling a press conference or making an announcement at some public event.

Some examples of presidential initiatives by President Clinton were:
- health-care reform
- welfare reform
- anti-crime legislation
- gun control legislation
- reform of the social security system

2 Submit the annual budget

The annual federal budget is drawn up for the president by the Office of Management and Budget (see section D.4). The president then submits it to Congress. This is followed by a lengthy bargaining process between the president and Congress — especially lengthy if the president and Congress are controlled by different political parties.

3 Sign legislation

Once bills have passed through a lengthy and complicated process in Congress (see Topic 5.F), they land on the president's desk. He has a number of options, but the most likely is that of signing the bill into law. He will do this to bills for which he wishes to take some credit. Elaborate bill-signing ceremonies are often held, attended by House and Senate members who have been particularly supportive, as well as interested parties who will be affected by the new legislation.

4 Veto legislation

As well as signing bills into law, the president has the option of vetoing them. The **regular veto** is a much-used presidential weapon. Even the threat of it can be an important bargaining tool. Table 6.2 shows the use of the veto by recent presidents. Altogether, from George Washington through to the end of the presidency of Bill Clinton, presidents have used over 2,500 regular vetoes.

The presidency

President	Regular vetoes used	Vetoes overridden
John Kennedy	12	0
Lyndon Johnson	16	0
Richard Nixon	26	7
Gerald Ford	48	12
Jimmy Carter	13	2
Ronald Reagan	39	9
George Bush	29	1
Bill Clinton	36	2
George W. Bush*	0	0

*to January 2005

Table 6.2 Regular vetoes and overrides, 1961–2005

To veto a bill, the president must:
- **veto the whole bill**, not just parts of it
- return the bill to the house which first considered it, within ten working days
- include a note explaining any objections

> This note is called the 'veto message'.

It is then up to Congress to decide what to do. Congress may decide to:
- do nothing — conceding that the president has won and the bill will not become law
- attempt to override the president's veto

> It is important to say 'a two-thirds majority in both houses'. To say 'a two-thirds majority in Congress' is at best misleading.

> They will judge this by looking at the 'final passage' vote in each house to see how small or large the majority was.

If Congress decides to attempt to override the president's veto then the bill must be given a **two-thirds** majority vote **in both houses of Congress.** This is exceedingly difficult to achieve. Of the 36 regular vetoes that Bill Clinton used, Congress was able to override only 2 of them. Of the over 2,500 regular vetoes used by presidents in over 200 years, only just over 100 of them have been overridden by Congress. This represents just 4%. But remember two important points. If Congress knows it cannot override the president's veto, it may well have given concessions to him whilst the bill was going through the legislative process. Furthermore, presidents will often choose not to veto bills if they know that Congress will override them. To have a veto overridden by Congress is politically damaging, especially if — as in the case of Jimmy Carter — it is inflicted by a Congress controlled by the president's own party. Table 6.3 gives examples of some of Bill Clinton's regular vetoes, including the two overridden by Congress.

Bill	Final House vote	Final Senate vote	Vetoed by president	House vote to override veto	Senate vote to override veto	Result
Securities Bill	**325–99**	**65–30**	**19 December 1995**	**319–100**	**68–30**	**Overridden**
Defense Budget 1996	267–149	51–43	28 December 1995	240–156	–	Sustained
Late-Term Abortion Ban	286–129	54–44	10 April 1996	285–137	57–41	Sustained
Disaster Relief Bill	220–201	67–31	9 June 1997	–	–	Sustained
Late-Term Abortion Ban	295–136	64–36	10 October 1997	296–132	64–36	Sustained
Military construction budget	**352–64**	**69–30**	**13 November 1997**	**347–69**	**78–20**	**Overridden**
Education Savings Accounts	225–197	59–36	21 July 1998	–	–	Sustained
1999 Tax Cut	221–206	50–49	23 September 1999	–	–	Sustained
Nuclear Waste Storage	253–167	64–34	25 April 2000	–	64–35	Sustained

Table 6.3 Clinton's regular vetoes: selected examples

The powers of the president

The president may also have the power of **pocket veto** at his disposal. But this can be used only after a session of Congress has adjourned. When Congress is in session, a bill becomes law after ten working days if the president neither signs nor vetoes it. But when Congress has adjourned and the president does not sign the bill, the bill is lost. This is called a pocket veto. Because Congress is no longer in session, pocket vetoes cannot be overridden. President Clinton used only one pocket veto during his 8 years — in December 2000, when he pocket-vetoed a consumer bankruptcy overhaul bill. President Reagan used 39 pocket vetoes during his 8 years in office and President George Bush used 17 during his 4 years.

5 Act as chief executive

The opening words of Article II of the Constitution state that: 'The executive power shall be vested in a president of the United States of America.' This makes the president the chief executive, in charge of running the executive branch of the federal government. This is a huge job and much of the day-to-day running is delegated to those who run the principal departments and agencies of the federal government (see section B of this topic).

6 Nominate executive branch officials

The State Department is the US equivalent of the UK's Foreign Office.

The president is given the power to nominate hundreds of officials to the executive branch of the federal government. The most important of these are the heads of the 15 executive departments such as State, Treasury and Agriculture. At the beginning of his second term, George W. Bush nominated Condoleezza Rice to be Secretary of State, Margaret Spellings to be Secretary of Education and Michael Johanns to be Secretary of Agriculture. All of these, of course, had to be confirmed by the Senate by simple majority vote.

The Attorney General heads the Justice Department.

Nominee	Post	Year appointed	Senate vote
Condoleezza Rice	Secretary of State	2005	85–13
Donald Rumsfeld	Secretary of Defense	2001	Voice vote
John Snow	Secretary of the Treasury	2003	Voice vote
Michael Johanns	Secretary of Agriculture	2005	Voice vote
Gale Norton	Secretary of the Interior	2001	75–24
Alberto Gonzales	Attorney General	2005	60–36
Carlos Gutierrez	Secretary of Commerce	2005	Voice vote
Elaine Chao	Secretary of Labor	2001	Voice vote
Michael Leavitt	Secretary of Health & Human Services	2005	Voice vote
Margaret Spellings	Secretary of Education	2005	Voice vote
Alphonso Jackson	Secretary of Housing & Urban Development	2004	Voice vote
Norman Mineta	Secretary of Transportation	2001	100–0
Samuel Bodman	Secretary of Energy	2005	Voice vote
Jim Nicholson	Secretary of Veterans' Affairs	2005	Voice vote
Michael Chertoff	Secretary of Homeland Security	2005	98–0

Table 6.4 George W. Bush's Cabinet nominees and confirmation votes, 2005

7   *Nominate judges*

Again, this involves the president in making hundreds of appointments. Not only must he fill up vacancies on the Supreme Court, he must also do this for the trial and appeal courts of the federal government. All judicial appointments are for life and therefore assume a special importance. And the most important are those to the Supreme Court (see Topic 8.A). During his 8 years in office, President Clinton appointed two members to the Supreme Court, Ruth Bader Ginsburg and Stephen Breyer. At the time of writing, there are still appointees of Presidents Nixon (1969–74) and Ford (1974–77) on the Supreme Court.

8   *Act as commander-in-chief*

This was a particularly significant power for the presidents in office between the 1940s and the early 1990s — from Franklin Roosevelt to George Bush. With the USA fighting in the Second World War and then taking the lead for the West in the Cold War, the president's commander-in-chief role was highly significant during a period that also saw the Korean War, the Vietnam War and the Gulf War — to name only the principal conflicts. Arguably, in the post-Cold War era, this power is less to the fore. But crises will still occur and the power is potentially an important one. Again, the president is checked by Congress's 'power of the purse', its power to declare war and to conduct investigations.

The events of 11 September 2001 clearly showed that.

9   *Negotiate treaties*

The president's seal of office shows an eagle clutching a bundle of arrows in one claw, symbolising the commander-in-chief role, and an olive branch in the other to symbolise his peace-making role. Modern-day presidents have used this power to negotiate such treaties as the Panama Canal Treaty (Jimmy Carter), the Strategic Arms Reduction Treaty (Ronald Reagan) and the Chemical Weapons Ban (George Bush).

Again, the president's power is checked by the Senate's power to ratify treaties. Table 6.5 shows that during the twentieth century, the Senate rejected treaties negotiated by the president on seven occasions. The 1999 occasion was the only one in which the treaty failed to gain even a simple majority, let alone the two-thirds majority required for ratification.

Date	President	Treaty	Senate vote (yes–no)
19 March 1920	Woodrow Wilson	Treaty of Versailles	49–35
18 January 1927	Calvin Coolidge	Commercial rights	50–34
14 March 1934	Franklin Roosevelt	St Lawrence Seaway	46–42
29 January 1935	Franklin Roosevelt	World Court	52–36
26 March 1960	Dwight Eisenhower	Law of Sea Convention	49–30
8 March 1983	Ronald Reagan	Montreal Protocol	50–42
13 October 1999	Bill Clinton	Comprehensive Test Ban	48–51

Table 6.5 Senate rejection of treaties, 1920–99

10 Pardon

Presidents possess the power of pardon. Mostly used in uncontroversial cases, this power has occasionally been used in high-profile and controversial ones. The most notable was President Ford's 1974 pardon of former President Richard Nixon. President George Bush caused controversy with his 1992 pardon of former Defense Secretary Caspar Weinberger, as did President Clinton over a number of pardons on his last day in office in January 2001.

B The federal bureaucracy

1 Twentieth-century expansion

Executive departments are also called 'cabinet departments' because their heads make up the president's cabinet.

With the expansion of the federal government (see Topic 1.E.4), the federal bureaucracy has grown hugely. Under George Washington, there were just three **executive departments** — State, War (later renamed Defense) and Treasury. By the time Theodore Roosevelt became president at the beginning of the twentieth century, a further three had been added — Interior, Justice and Agriculture. But that century saw another nine departments added. These included such areas as Health, Housing and Urban Development, Transportation and Energy. By 2005, there were 15 executive departments (see Table 6.6).

Executive department	Created
State	1789
Treasury	1789
Defense	1949
Justice	1870
Interior	1849
Agriculture	1889
Commerce	1903
Labor	1903
Health and Human Services	1953
Housing and Urban Development	1965
Transportation	1966
Energy	1977
Education	1979
Veterans' Affairs	1989
Homeland Security	2002

Table 6.6 Executive departments and dates created

2 The size and scale of today's bureaucracy

But that is not all. Add to that the huge number of **executive agencies** and **regulatory commissions**. Today these number in the region of 60 and include

such bodies as the National Aeronautics and Space Administration (NASA), the Central Intelligence Agency (CIA), the Environmental Protection Agency (EPA) and the Federal Election Commission (FEC).

Together, the departments, agencies and commissions have some 3 million civilian employees. (Add another 2 million for the military.) And, needless to say, these 3 million civil servants do not all work in Washington DC. The federal bureaucracy is spread throughout the entire USA. There are federal government offices in every good-sized US city. In 1995, it was the **federal government** building in Oklahoma City that was the target of a major act of terrorism.

This is why the president has such a difficult job running the federal bureaucracy. It is big and it is spread across 4,500 km and four time zones. And don't forget also that many federal government programmes are dependent upon implementation by **state governments**. Former President Jimmy Carter commented: 'Before I became president, I was warned that dealing with the federal bureaucracy would be one of the worst problems I would have to face. It has been even worse than I had anticipated.'

C The cabinet

1 Definition and membership

Another 'scholarly' quotation for your essays.

The president's cabinet is not mentioned in the Constitution. According to presidential scholar Richard Fenno, it is **'institutionalised by usage alone'**. In other words, 'it's used because it's used!' The cabinet is an **advice-giving group** selected by the president to aid him in making decisions, membership of which is determined both by tradition and presidential discretion. By tradition, it is made up of the heads of the 15 executive departments. By presidential discretion, others can be given 'cabinet rank'. These might include the US ambassador to the United Nations and the US trade representative.

2 Cabinet recruitment

This is one of those topics where illuminating comparisons from UK politics should definitely be made.

You can use the term 'cabinet officers' but not 'cabinet ministers'.

Unlike an incoming British prime minister, a newly elected US president such as George W. Bush does not have a 'shadow cabinet' ready and waiting to form the new administration. And, unlike in the British parliamentary system, where cabinet members are drawn from the legislature, members of the US president's cabinet cannot be currently serving members of Congress. Between 1961 and 2005, fewer than one in five cabinet officers had any previous experience in Congress. Amongst George W. Bush's original 14 heads of departments in 2001, only 4 had any congressional experience. Members of the president's cabinet will therefore come from a very diverse background. These are likely to include:

- Congress, but these must be either former members or those willing to resign their seats (e.g. former senator John Ashcroft as head of the Justice

The cabinet

Department in the new cabinet of George W. Bush, who had just been defeated in the 2000 Senate elections)

- state governors (e.g. Governor Tommy Thompson of Wisconsin as head of the Health and Human Services Department in George W. Bush's first term)
- city mayors (e.g. Clinton's Secretary of Transportation, Federico Peña, had been Mayor of Denver)
- academics (e.g. Rod Paige, George W. Bush's first term Education Secretary, has been a professor at the University of Cincinnati)

It is also highly likely that cabinet members will be policy specialists. Again, here are three such examples from the initial cabinet of President George W. Bush:

- Rod Paige (Education Secretary) — Superintendent of Public Schools in Houston, Texas, 1994–2000.
- Anthony Principi (Veterans' Affairs Secretary) — a Vietnam War veteran.
- Condoleezza Rice (Secretary of State) — former National Security Adviser.

Because most cabinet members are policy specialists, there are no such things in US politics as 'cabinet reshuffles', those great bonanzas of speculation that exist in UK politics. Over the last 45 years (1961–2005), only 11 cabinet officers have ever headed more than one department. Some examples are given in Table 6.7.

Cabinet officer	Departments headed	President	Years
Elliot Richardson	Health	Nixon	1970–73
	Defense	Nixon	January–April 1973
	Justice	Nixon	May–October 1973
	Commerce	Ford	1976–77
George Shultz	Labor	Nixon	1969–70
	Treasury	Nixon	1972–74
	State	Reagan	1982–89
James Baker	Treasury	Reagan	1985–88
	State	Bush	1989–92
Elizabeth Dole	Transportation	Reagan	1983–87
	Labor	Bush	1989–91
Federico Peña	Transportation	Clinton	1993–97
	Energy	Clinton	1997–98
Norman Mineta	Commerce	Clinton	2000–01
	Transportation	George W. Bush	2001–

Table 6.7 Cabinet officers who have headed more than one department: selected examples

Presidents also like to balance their cabinet in terms of geographic region, race, gender, ideology and age. Incoming President Clinton in 1993 even went so far as to talk about having a cabinet that 'looked like America'. President George W. Bush included in his first Cabinet:

- a Lebanese-American (Spencer Abraham)
- two African-Americans (Colin Powell and Rod Paige)
- a Chinese-American (Eliane Chao)
- a Japanese-American (Norman Mineta)

All cabinet appointments have to be confirmed by a simple majority vote of the Senate. The last time the Senate rejected a president's cabinet appointee was in

1989, when they rejected John Tower, George Bush's nominee to head the Defense Department. In 2005, Alberto Gonzales was confirmed by 60 votes to 36 (see Table 6.4 for details).

3 Cabinet meetings

Meetings of the president with the full cabinet tend to get a pretty bad press. Many who have attended them describe them as boring and a waste of time. Indeed, some presidents have held very few. Most presidents have held cabinet meetings only about once a month. Clinton managed only two or three a year, whilst at the other extreme both Presidents Carter and Reagan held 36 meetings in their first year in office. The number of meetings tends to decline as the administration wears on. There are three principal reasons for this:

(1) Some of the functions of the cabinet are no longer applicable.

(2) The president has increasing calls on his time, not least when he has to run for re-election. Jimmy Carter managed only six cabinet meetings in his final year in office.

(3) Presidents tend to become disillusioned with their cabinet officers, often believing them to be disloyal. In the words of Nixon White House aide John Ehrlichman, the cabinet go off and 'marry the natives'.

'The natives' being the bureaucrats in their own departments.

And cabinet meetings have had some fairly poor reviews. Consider the following selection:

- 'The President listened to the group with thinly disguised impatience.' (J. Edward Day, Kennedy cabinet member)

Some 'original' quotations. Good essay material!

- 'I always went to cabinet meetings thinking, "I wonder how soon I can get away from this so I can get on with all the work I've got to do." And I think most of my colleagues had the same idea.' (A Johnson cabinet member)
- 'Nothing of substance was discussed. There was no disagreement because there was nothing to disagree about. Things over which one might have disagreed were not discussed.' (Elliot Richardson, a Nixon cabinet member)
- 'Carter cabinet meetings were almost useless. The discussions were desultory. There was no coherent theme to them, and after a while they were held less and less frequently.' (Zbigniew Brzezinski, National Security Advisor to President Carter)
- 'Very often they were a waste of time. You could get very bored.' (A member of President George Bush's cabinet)

Nonetheless, cabinet meetings can perform useful functions, both for the president and for cabinet members. They can enable the president to:

- engender team spirit — especially at the beginning of his administration
- look collegial and consultative
- give information to all cabinet members
- glean information from cabinet members — find out what's going on in each department

This is the main function of George W. Bush's cabinet meetings.

- debate policies
- present 'big picture' items such as the budget, tours, campaigns, initiatives
- check up on legislation going through Congress in which he has an interest
- see cabinet members he wouldn't otherwise see

Can you imagine a British cabinet minister claiming this as a function of meetings at Number 10? Hardly!

For cabinet members themselves, cabinet meetings serve:
- as get-to-know-you sessions — especially at the beginning of an administration when a number of cabinet colleagues may be total strangers
- to sort out inter-departmental disputes
- as a means of catching other members (before and/or after the meetings)
- as an opportunity to see the president — whom many of them wouldn't otherwise see
- to gain them prestige back at their department, with first-hand news of what the president wants

Not all cabinet members have rubbished the meetings. Consider the following:
- 'Cabinet meetings were often vigorous, such as the one on the pros and cons of building the Russian oil pipeline. It was quite a shouting match.' (Frank Carlucci, Defense Secretary to President Reagan)
- 'At the meeting prior to the Malta Summit [with Soviet President Gorbachev in December 1989], for example, the President engaged the cabinet in a very significant discussion of foreign policy. I think the cabinet valued the opportunity to present their views directly and candidly. It allowed the President to broaden his consultations.' (Michael Jackson, member of President George Bush's Office of Cabinet Affairs)

4 Cabinet councils

One of the main problems associated with full cabinet meetings is that because members are likely to be policy specialists, many will find policy-specific agenda items — other than those in their area — of no interest at all. To get round this problem, some recent presidents have developed a series of more policy-specific cabinet councils. These existed during the presidencies of Ronald Reagan, George Bush and George W. Bush. There are currently three in existence in the latter administration:
- The Economic Policy Council
- The Domestic Policy Council
- The National Security Council

As a result, full cabinet meetings are held less frequently and tend to be reserved for 'team talks' by the president at key moments in the political calendar — just before a State of the Union address, a budget proposal, a foreign tour, an election cycle.

For example, the mid-term Congressional elections (2002) or the run-up to the 2004 presidential election.

5 Relations with the Executive Office of the President

It must be remembered that the principal job of cabinet officers is not to act as presidential advisors. There are good reasons why not:
- They have huge departments to run.
- They are not based in the White House.
- They have loyalties other than those to the president.

The latter often leads to accusations of disloyalty from those whose principal function it *is* to act as 'all the president's men', i.e. the members of the Executive

Office of the President (EXOP), which includes the White House staff (see section D). For whilst members of EXOP serve only the president, cabinet members must bear in mind the wishes of Congress (whose votes decide their departmental budgets), their own departmental bureaucracy, as well as interest groups which have important links with their department. Unlike the Cabinet, members of EXOP enjoy close proximity and access to the president.

Presidential scholar Richard Neustadt has written recently: '[An incoming president] must prepare the cabinet members against the shocking discovery that most of them are not the principal advisors to the president, are not going to be, and never will be, not since the White House staff has come into mature existence.'

6 The cabinet: important or unimportant?

How important is the cabinet? Individually very important, though some far more than others. They run huge executive departments and spend vast budgets. But collectively, the cabinet can never be *that* important. There are six main reasons for this:

(1) Article II of the Constitution states that 'all executive power shall be vested in a president'.

(2) There is no doctrine of collective responsibility.

(3) The president is not 'first among equals' — he is just 'first'. As Anthony King has stated: 'He doesn't sum up at the end of the meeting; he *is* the meeting.'

(4) Cabinet officers are not his political rivals; they are not about to become president.

(5) They have a problem of divided loyalty as well as a lack of proximity and access to the president.

(6) The president has EXOP, which is important in helping and advising him to achieve his goals.

'The very nature of the cabinet — a body with no constitutional standing, members with no independent political base of their own and no requirement that the president seeks or follows their advice — helps contribute to its lack of influence as a collective body.' (Professor Michael Genovese)

D The Executive Office of the President

1 Definition and membership

The Executive Office of the President is an umbrella term for an organisation that consists of the top presidential staff agencies that provide help, advice, coordination and administrative support for the president.

Created in 1939, after the **Brownlow Committee** reported that **'the president needs help'**, EXOP has grown to include around a dozen or so offices. The most important ones are:

This is sometimes abbreviated to EOP.

These three — Congress, the bureaucracy, pressure groups — are sometimes referred to as 'the iron triangle'.

In essays, it is very important to make clear the distinction between the cabinet *as individuals* and the cabinet *as a collectivity*.

Named after its chair, Dr Louis Brownlow.

- the White House staff
- the National Security Council
- the Office of Management and Budget

Why did presidents from the mid-twentieth century 'need help' in running the federal government? There were three main reasons:
- The huge increase in the size and scale of the federal government caused by nineteenth-century westward expansion and industrialisation.
- The 'New Deal' programme introduced by FDR to help cure the effects of the Depression.
- The USA's newly found role as a world power.

2 The White House staff

The White House staff includes the president's most trusted and closest aides and advisors, such as:
- Press Secretary (Scott McClellan)
- Chief of Staff (Andrew Card)
- Deputy Chief of Staff (Karl Rove)

The principal function of the White House staff is to provide advice and administrative support for the president on a daily basis. This will involve:
- policy advice
- personnel management
- crisis management
- liaison with the federal bureaucracy
- liaison with Congress
- running the White House
- deciding and executing the president's daily schedule
- acting as 'lightning conductors' for the president
- ensuring an orderly decision-making process for the president

Members of the White House staff are meant to act not as policy-makers, but as **'honest brokers'**. They are not meant to be always in the media spotlight, but to have something of a **'passion for anonymity'**. As then White House Chief of Staff Dick Cheney stated of his relationship with President Ford: 'He takes the credit; I take the blame.'

The role of the **White House chief of staff** is the most critical. Some (e.g. 'Mack' McLarty, 1993–94) have been overwhelmed by the job, possibly because of their own lack of Washington experience. Others (e.g. John Sununu, 1989–92) became far too obtrusive and wanted to become a kind of 'deputy president'. The best model is that of the 'honest broker', 'salesman' and 'javelin catcher' for the president, played well by such people as Dick Cheney (Ford), James Baker (Reagan) and Leon Panetta (Clinton).

The phrase 'javelin catcher' is attributed to Carter's Chief of Staff, Jack Watson.

3 The National Security Council

Created in 1947, the National Security Council (NSC) was established to help the president coordinate foreign and defence policy. Headed by the National Security

Advisor (NSA), the NSC began life as an in-house think-tank for the president. The NSC would gather information, advice and policy options from groups such as:

Also known as the Pentagon, after the huge five-sided building that houses it.

- the State Department
- the Defense Department
- the Central Intelligence Agency (CIA)
- relevant congressional committees (e.g. Senate Foreign Relations Committee)
- the Joint Chiefs of Staff
- US ambassadors around the world

The NSC would then act as 'honest broker' and 'policy coordinator' to present carefully argued options ready for presidential decision-making.

President Nixon greatly increased the role of the NSA when he appointed Henry Kissinger to the post. Kissinger became a roving foreign policy-maker for the president, largely cutting out the State Department and other agencies, becoming a policy player rather than a mere facilitator. But this new enhanced role for the NSA caused grave problems for both Presidents Carter (over the Iranian hostage crisis) and Reagan (over the Iran-Contra affair). Subsequent NSAs, such as Brent Scowcroft (Bush), Sandy Berger (Clinton) and Condoleezza Rice (George W. Bush), have reverted to the more traditional role.

4 *The Office of Management and Budget*

This was created in 1970 by President Nixon, when he revamped the then Bureau of the Budget.

The two principal functions of the Office of Management and Budget (OMB) are:
(1) to advise the president on the allocation of federal funds in the annual budget
(2) to oversee the spending of all federal government departments and agencies

It is headed by the OMB director, just about the only EXOP post that does require Senate confirmation. Some former OMB directors, such as Leon Panetta for Bill Clinton (1993–94), have provided first-class help and advice for the president on financial and budget matters. Others have proved politically embarrassing (Reagan's David Stockman) or have led the president down disastrous paths (Bush's Richard Darman, who in 1990 advised the President that breaking his 'no new taxes' pledge would not be politically costly in his re-election bid in 2 years' time!).

Darman was known by his critics as 'the prince of darkness'.

E Relations with Congress

Almost every power that the president possesses is checked by Congress. The president, therefore, needs Congress's agreement. But in a system of 'separated institutions, sharing powers' (Neustadt), this is by no means easy. And party links do not help much either. The president and the majority of Congress may be of different parties. This has certainly been the case in recent decades, as is shown in Table 6.8.

Years	President	House	Senate
1969–70	Republican: Nixon	Democrat 243–192	Democrat 57–43
1971–72	Republican: Nixon	Democrat 255–180	Democrat 55–45
1973–74	Republican: Nixon/Ford	Democrat 244–191	Democrat 57–43
1975–76	Republican: Ford	Democrat 291–144	Democrat 62–38
1977–78	**Democrat: Carter**	**Democrat 291–143**	**Democrat 62–38**
1979–80	**Democrat: Carter**	**Democrat 276–159**	**Democrat 59–41**
1981–82	Republican: Reagan	Democrat 243–192	Republican 53–47
1983–84	Republican: Reagan	Democrat 269–166	Republican 54–46
1985–86	Republican: Reagan	Democrat 253–182	Republican 53–47
1987–88	Republican: Reagan	Democrat 258–177	Democrat 55–45
1989–90	Republican: Bush	Democrat 260–175	Democrat 55–45
1991–92	Republican: Bush	Democrat 267–167	Democrat 56–44
1993–94	**Democrat: Clinton**	**Democrat 258–176**	**Democrat 58–42**
1995–96	Democrat: Clinton	Republican 230–204	Republican 54–46
1997–98	Democrat: Clinton	Republican 227–220	Republican 55–45
1999–2000	Democrat: Clinton	Republican 223–211	Republican 55–45
Jan.–May 2001	**Republican: G. W. Bush**	**Republican 222–212**	**Republican 50–50**
June 2001–02	Republican: G. W. Bush	Republican 221–212	Democrat 50–49
2003–04	**Republican: G. W. Bush**	**Republican 229–205**	**Republican 51–48**
2005	**Republican: G. W. Bush**	**Republican 232–202**	**Republican 55–44**

Table 6.8 Party control of Congress and the presidency, 1969–2005

And even when the two branches are controlled by the same party, this is no guarantee of action — witness the difficulties Bill Clinton experienced in his failed attempt to pass his health-care reforms in 1993–94. As Richard Neustadt has stated: 'What the Constitution separates, the political parties do not combine.'

But the president needs Congress. For, as Table 6.9 shows, without it he can do little or nothing. This is all part of the intricate system of 'checks and balances' devised by the Founding Fathers (see Topic 1.D). Professor S. E. Finer has likened the president and Congress to 'two halves of a bank note, each useless without the other.' And the Founding Fathers' desire for cooperation and compromise ('ambition must counteract ambition', as James Madison put it) often leads to inaction and gridlock.

> What the Constitution separates is, of course, the three branches of the federal government.

> What Madison meant by this was that the 'ambition' of the President (i.e. what he wants to do) must be checked by the 'ambition' of Congress (i.e. what it wants to do) and vice versa.

Powers of the president	Checks by Congress
Propose legislation	Amend/block legislation
Submit the annual budget	Amend budget
Veto legislation	Override veto
Nominate executive officials (e.g. cabinet)	**Senate's** power of confirmation
Nominate federal judges	**Senate's** power of confirmation
Negotiate treaties	**Senate's** power of ratification
Commander-in-chief of the armed forces	Declare war/power of the purse
Act as chief executive	Investigation/impeachment/trial/removal

Table 6.9 Powers of the president and checks by Congress

Thus, presidents cannot rely on **formal powers** alone to get what they want, helpful as these may be. They must also use **informal powers** of persuasion. As Richard Neustadt so succinctly puts it: **'The president's power is the power to persuade.'**

1 *Methods of presidential persuasion*

'I sit here all day trying to persuade people to do the things they ought to have sense enough to do without my persuading them....That's all the powers of the president amount to', famously commented a frustrated President Harry Truman. But Truman was right. So how does a president persuade? There are two methods — through people and through perks.

1.1 Persuasion through people

The president, if he is to be a successful persuader, must work through a number of other people. He cannot — nor should he — try to do it all himself. Who can he use?

- **The vice-president:** as presiding officer of the Senate, he has a foothold in Congress.
- His own **congressional liaison staff:** these are members of the White House staff who work as full-time lobbyists for the president in Congress.
- **Cabinet officers:** each of these works in their own policy-related areas.
- **Party leaders** in Congress, including the House Speaker, Majority and Minority Leaders in both houses, whips, committee chairs and ranking minority members (see Topic 5.D).

All of the last five VPs (Mondale, Bush, Quayle, Gore and Cheney) have formerly been members of Congress, which also helps.

1.2 Persuasion through perks

This works hand-in-hand with the people mentioned above. The president may:

- make **phone calls** to selected members of Congress
- **offer help with legislation** that benefits members' constituents
- **offer help with federal executive/judicial appointments** of interest to constituents
- **invite members to a meeting** at the White House
- **go to Capitol Hill** to address a selected group of members
- **offer to campaign** for members of his own party

Capitol Hill, in Washington DC, is where the building housing Congress stands.

And if all else fails, the president can go on national television to **appeal over the heads of members of Congress** directly to the people. This is what President Johnson called 'putting Congress's feet to the fire'.

2 *The results of presidential persuasion*

David Mervin has described the US president as **'bargainer-in-chief'** — and he is. But after all is said and done, the president will be hoping that it will result in

his legislation being passed, his appointments confirmed and his treaties ratified. The president's success rate is measured each year in what is called **the presidential support score** (see Table 6.10). This statistic measures how often the president won in roll-call votes in the House and Senate in which he took a clear position, expressed as a percentage of the whole.

Year	President	Support score (%)
1993	Clinton	86.4
1994	Clinton	86.4
1995	Clinton	36.2
1996	Clinton	55.2
1997	Clinton	53.6
1998	Clinton	50.6
1999	Clinton	37.8
2000	Clinton	55.0
2001	Bush	87.0
2002	Bush	87.8
2003	Bush	78.7
2004	Bush	72.5

Table 6.10 Presidential support score, 1993–2004

Although the presidential support score is a useful guide to presidential success, keep in mind that:
- the score does not measure the importance of votes
- presidents can avoid low scores by just simply not taking positions on votes they expect to lose
- the score does not count bills which fail even to come to a vote on the floor of either house (e.g. Clinton's health-care reform bill never came to a vote in either house in 1994 and therefore did not feature in the 86.4% support score recorded that year)

It is also worth keeping in mind that changes in Congress — and more widely in the US political system — make the president's job more difficult these days when trying to build support for his legislation than was the case, say, back in the 1950s and 1960s. There are five reasons for this:

(1) Declining levels of party discipline in Congress.

(2) Less likelihood that the president and a majority of Congress will be of the same party.

(3) House and Senate members being more aware of constituents' wishes (through the effects of C-SPAN and e-mail, for example) and therefore perhaps less willing to go along with what the president wants.

(4) Changes in the methods of selecting presidential candidates, resulting in 'Washington outsiders' becoming president — Governors Carter, Reagan, Clinton and George W. Bush.

(5) The fragmentation of power in Congress, including the declining power of committee chairs and the like.

C-SPAN is the cable television company which gives complete coverage of House and Senate debates.

F Limits on presidential power

Consider the following comments:

- 'Weakness is still what I see; weakness in the sense of a great gap between what is expected of a man (or someday woman) and assured capacity to carry through.' (Richard Neustadt)
- 'The presidency is not a powerful office....Presidents cannot command obedience to their wishes but must persuade.' (James Pfiffner)
- 'It sometimes seems almost miraculous that presidents accomplish anything at all.' (David Mervin)
- 'Leadership is difficult precisely because the framers of the Constitution wanted it to be so....Opportunities to check power abound; opportunities to exercise power are limited.' (Thomas Cronin and Michael Genovese)

Not exactly a vote of confidence for 'the most powerful person in the world' claim! But the more you realise the **limits** on presidential power, the better will be your understanding of the paradoxes of the office of the US presidency.

What are these limits? They can be grouped under eight headings.

1 Congress

Congress can amend/block/delay the president's bills and override his vetoes; the Senate can refuse to confirm his appointments or ratify his treaties; and Congress can investigate, impeach and try him — even remove him from office. (See Topic 5.B.)

2 Supreme Court

The Supreme Court can declare the president's actions — and those of any member of the executive branch — unconstitutional. Consider the following three examples:

- ***Youngstown Sheet and Tube Company v. Sawyer* (1952):** the Court declared unconstitutional the actions of President Truman's Commerce Secretary Charles Sawyer in ordering troops to break a steel strike.
- ***United States v. Richard M. Nixon* (1974):** the Court declared that President Nixon's refusal to hand over the 'White House tapes' — concerning the Watergate affair — was unconstitutional.
- ***William Jefferson Clinton v. Paula Corbin Jones* (1997):** the Court declared that President Clinton had to face charges of sexual harassment made by Ms Jones whilst he was still president, rather than waiting until he left office.

It was this case that led to President Clinton having to answer questions posed by Ms Jones's lawyers in January 1998, including ones concerning a possible relationship between the President and a White House employee named Monica Lewinsky. The rest, as they say, is history!

3 Public opinion

President Clinton discovered how important public opinion was to being president. He survived his many scandals mainly because his public opinion ratings remained high. President Nixon saw the other side of that coin.

4 Pressure groups

Pressure groups can mobilise public opinion either for or against the president himself or his policies. (See Topic 4.)

5 The media

All modern-day presidents live in an era where the media can profoundly limit what they can do — ask Johnson about Vietnam or Clinton about health-care reform. The media's coverage of the president as a person is also critical.

6 The federal bureaucracy

The president is only one person in an executive branch made up of 14 executive departments, some 60 other federal government agencies, boards and commissions employing some 3 million civil servants. Getting the federal bureaucracy to *do* things can be a challenge to any president.

7 Federalism

And it's not just the federal government that limits the president. Many federal government programmes are implemented by state and local governments across the entire USA.

8 Other factors

The president is also often limited by such factors as:
- his own professional reputation
- the quality of his staff
- the unity (or otherwise) of his party and of the opposition
- crises (or the lack of them)
- luck

In an article in *The Economist* in March 2001, Vice-President Dick Cheney was described as 'the most powerful vice-president in history'.

Article II of the Constitution states that 'in case of the removal of the President from office, or of his death, resignation or inability to discharge the powers and duties of the said office, the same shall devolve on the Vice-President'. That the vice-president may become president gives the office its potential importance. But throughout most of the nineteenth and a good deal of the twentieth century, the office seemed to be a dumping ground for political non-entities — the has-beens, might-have-beens and thought-they-ought-to-have-beens of US politics. The list, after all, does include Hannibal Hamblin (1861–65) and Schuyler Colfax (1869–73). But no longer. In Washington circles today, Vice-President Cheney has quickly been dubbed 'the prime minister'. But Cheney is not the first important vice-president. The office has been growing in importance for decades. In this topic, we shall discover both why and how.

The topic is divided into the following two major headings:

A Selection, election and powers
B The increased importance of the office: why and how

A Selection, election and powers

1 Selection of vice-presidential candidates

The selection of the vice-presidential candidate is now done **by the presidential candidate** at — or nowadays usually just before — the party's National Convention (see Topic 2.A.3.2b). Times were when the National Convention itself did the choosing. But this has not occurred in either major party since 1956.

In 1956, Adlai Stevenson allowed the Democratic Convention to choose his running-mate, Senator Estes Kefauver of Tennessee.

In order to be chosen, the vice-presidential candidate must fulfil the same constitutional requirements as for the presidency regarding age, citizenship and residency, and not have already served two terms as president. This is for the simple reason that the vice-president may be called upon to become president.

2 Election of the vice-president

Again, the system has changed. Between 1789 and 1801, the vice-president was elected separately from the president. When the Electoral College votes were counted (see Topic 2.A.5), the winner would become president and the runner-up would become vice-president. This is how the first three vice-presidents — John Adams (1789–97), Thomas Jefferson (1797–1801) and Aaron Burr (1801–05) — were elected. The office was therefore seen as being **'the president in waiting'**. Adams, the first vice-president, became the second president. Jefferson, the second vice-president, became the third president.

The next vice-president to achieve this feat was George Bush in 1989.

But in 1804, the **12th Amendment** was ratified. From then on, the president and vice-president were elected together — a **'joint ticket'**. The importance of the office declined drastically. Of the next 32 vice-presidents, only one — Martin Van Buren in 1837 — was elected president in his own right, other than those who first came to the office by the death of the president.

3 Appointment of the vice-president

In 1967, another constitutional amendment was passed affecting the office of the vice-presidency. The **25th Amendment**, amongst other things, gave the president the power to fill up vacancies in the vice-presidency. As Table 7.1 shows, for much of the nineteenth and twentieth centuries, the office remained empty. Either the vice-president himself died or the president died and the vice-president became president. Indeed, in the last 50 years of the nineteenth century, there was a vice-president in office for little more than half the time!

Dates	Reason for the vice-presidency being vacant
1812–13	Vice-President George Clinton died in office
1814–17	Vice-President Elbridge Gerry died in office
1832–33	Vice-President John Calhoun resigned to become a US senator
1841–45	President Harrison died; **VP John Tyler became president**
1850–53	President Taylor died; **VP Millard Fillmore became president**
1853–57	Vice-President William King died in office
1865–69	President Lincoln assassinated; **VP Andrew Johnson became president**
1875–77	Vice-President Henry Wilson died in office
1881–85	President Garfield assassinated; **VP Chester Arthur became president**
1885–89	Vice-President Thomas Hendricks died in office
1899–1901	Vice-President Garret Hobart died in office
1901–05	President McKinley assassinated; **VP Theodore Roosevelt became president**
1912–13	Vice-President James Sherman died in office
1923–25	President Harding died; **VP Calvin Coolidge became president**
1945–49	President F. D. Roosevelt died; **VP Harry Truman became president**
1963–65	President Kennedy assassinated; **VP Lyndon Johnson became president**

Table 7.1 Vacancies in the vice-presidency, 1812–1965

Do make sure you say 'newly appointed' rather than 'elected'. Congress did not have to confirm Dick Cheney as vice-president in 2001 because he was elected.

This all changed with the 25th Amendment. When, in 1973, Vice-President Spiro Agnew resigned, President Nixon appointed Congressman Gerald Ford of Michigan to fill the post. Within less than a year, Nixon himself resigned over the Watergate affair. Ford became president and he appointed former New York Governor Nelson Rockefeller as the new vice-president. Newly appointed vice-presidents have to be confirmed by a vote in **both** houses of Congress. A simple majority is required in each house. This is the only appointment the House of Representatives gets to confirm.

In his absence, the task is performed by junior senators from the majority party.

On average, a vice-president can expect to cast a vote about once a year.

4 Constitutional powers

The vice-president has five constitutional powers:

(1) Presiding officer of the Senate: this power involves him in chairing Senate debates, though in practice he will rarely do this.

(2) Casting a vote in Senate in the case of a tie: in May 1999, Al Gore broke a 50–50 tied vote by voting in favour of an amendment to the Crime Bill that would require criminal background checks on all gun sales at gun shows. In April 2001, Dick Cheney used this power for the first time to help pass George W. Bush's $1.6 trillion tax cut.

(3) Counting the Electoral College votes and announcing the winner before a joint session of Congress: in January 2001, Vice-President Al Gore had to announce his own defeat in the Electoral College vote at the hands of Governor George W. Bush.

(4) Becoming president on the death, resignation or removal from office of the president: this has occurred nine times, eight times by the death of the president (see Table 7.1) and once when Nixon resigned (August 1974).

(5) Becoming acting president if the president is declared, or declares himself, disabled: a provision of the 25th Amendment (1967) used only once, when in July 1985 Vice-President George Bush became Acting President for 8 hours whilst President Reagan underwent surgery in a Washington hospital.

With the exception of the fourth power, they do not make an impressive list. The first vice-president, John Adams, famously commented of his office: **'In this I am nothing, but I may be everything.'** Others have been even less generous, describing the office as anything from 'not worth a bucket of warm spit' (John Nance Garner, 1933–41) to being 'as useful as a cow's fifth teat' (Harry Truman, 1945).

B The increased importance of the office: why and how

1 The period of unimportance

Certainly for much of the nineteenth century and the first half of the twentieth century, the office of vice-president was regarded as unimportant. Amongst the reasons for this were:
- its lack of significant powers
- the passage of the 12th Amendment, depriving the vice-president of election in his own right
- the frequency with which the office remained empty
- that between 1804 and the 1950s, it was not seen as an obvious stepping-stone to the presidency, whereas being a senator or a state governor were seen in that way

• that presidents were not especially over-burdened with the duties of their office and therefore gave little of significance to their vice-presidents to do.

One frustrated occupant of the office commented that he seemed to spend most of his time 'going to funerals', a reference to the fact that vice-presidents were often sent abroad to represent the president at foreign funerals.

2 The emergence of the 'modern vice-presidency'

The office of vice-president is clearly now more significant and prestigious than used to be the case. Why and how did this occur?

Some commentators suggest that the turning point was when Harry Truman became president on the death of FDR in 1945. He was shocked by how little he knew of what was going on in the White House. Admittedly, he had been vice-president for little more than 3 months when Roosevelt died, but he did not even know that the USA had developed a nuclear weapon. Truman was determined that never again would a vice-president be kept in such ignorance. The trouble was that for the next 4 years, Truman did not have a vice-president! But it was Truman's vice-president, Alben Barkley (1949–53), who became the first to attend cabinet meetings routinely. Truman also made him a member of the National Security Council.

> Later that same year, he used it!

However, the real change probably came with the Eisenhower–Nixon administration (1953–61). There are a number of reasons for this:
• Nixon was a nationally known figure before becoming vice-president.
• He was only the fifth vice-president to serve 8 years in the office.
• The role of the federal government, and thereby the role of the president, had increased significantly as a result of both Roosevelt's 'New Deal' policies and of the USA's new superpower status.
• President Eisenhower adopted a delegatory approach to the presidency.
• Eisenhower suffered from bouts of ill-health, including a 5-month lay-off recovering from a heart attack.

> In Venezuela, Nixon's motorcade was attacked by an angry, rock-throwing crowd.

As a result of this, during his 8 years as vice-president, Nixon:
• chaired 19 cabinet meetings in the president's absence
• visited 54 countries, including high-profile visits to Venezuela (1958) and the USSR (1959)
• came to be regarded as Eisenhower's successor, Eisenhower being the first president to be limited to two terms in office

> The 22nd Amendment introducing the two-term limit was ratified in 1951, but excluded the then-incumbent President Harry Truman.

From this point on, the office gradually emerged as more important and therefore more sought-after:
• **Lyndon Johnson** (1961–63) chaired the president's Commission on Employment Opportunities and took a leading role in progress on civil rights.
• **Hubert Humphrey** (1965–69) was used by Johnson as his major link with local government — Humphrey had been Mayor of Minneapolis — in the enactment of his 'Great Society' programme to improve life in the inner cities.
• **Spiro Agnew** (1969–73) — a former Baltimore City councillor and governor of Maryland — headed Nixon's Office of Intergovernmental Relations.

- **Walter Mondale** (1977–81) became a general policy advisor to President Carter and was the first vice-president to be given a West Wing office and to be shown the Presidential Daily Briefing (PDB) — the intelligence briefing given to the president at the start of each day.

All subsequent vice-presidents have benefited from this piece-by-piece growth in the importance of the office. All vice-presidents now attend cabinet meetings, sit on the NSC, have a West Wing office, see the PDB and so on. No longer is the office a dumping-ground for non-entities that it was in decades gone by. The passage of the 25th Amendment, resulting in the fact that the office will now always be occupied, has also had a role in enhancing the status of the office.

Vice-president	Dates	Subsequent political career
Richard Nixon	**1953–61**	**Republican presidential candidate 1960; president 1969–74**
Lyndon Johnson	**1961–63**	**President 1963–69**
Hubert Humphrey	1965–69	Democratic presidential candidate 1968
Spiro Agnew	1969–73	–
Gerald Ford	**1973–74**	**President 1974–77**
Nelson Rockefeller	1974–77	(Had contested Republican presidential primaries in 1968)
Walter Mondale	1977–81	Democratic presidential candidate 1984
George Bush	**1981–89**	**President 1989–93**
Dan Quayle	1989–93	–
Al Gore	1993–2001	Democratic presidential candidate 2000

Table 7.2 Subsequent political careers of the vice-presidents, from Nixon to Gore

As Table 7.2 shows, the last ten vice-presidents (not counting Dick Cheney) have included four presidents-to-be — Nixon, Johnson, Ford and George Bush. Of the remaining six, three became the presidential candidates of their party — Humphrey, Mondale and Gore. Another — Nelson Rockefeller — had previously run in the presidential primaries. That leaves only Spiro Agnew and Dan Quayle as vice-presidents who seem not to have been regarded by others as being of presidential quality.

Add to this fact that, of the last five presidents, four — Carter, Reagan, Clinton and George W. Bush — have been Washington 'outsiders'. They had never before held political office in Washington, serving only as state governors. Their respective vice-presidents — Mondale, George Bush, Gore and Cheney — were all Washington 'insiders'. It is this that gives Dick Cheney his importance in the Bush administration. Cheney — a former White House Chief of Staff, Congressman and Secretary of Defense — is seen as the person to help President George W. Bush get things done in Washington.

'It is no exaggeration to say that there is a new vice-presidency. [It is] a highly visible office that is increasingly recognised as a springboard to the presidency.' (Paul Light, *Vice Presidential Power*, 1984)

TOPIC 8 *The Supreme Court*

The third branch of the federal government is the judiciary, which enforces and interprets the law. There are three tiers of courts: the trial courts, the appeal courts and the Supreme Court. We need concern ourselves with only the Supreme Court.

The Supreme Court is important for two reasons. First, its **members hold office for life** and, second, its functions include not only interpreting federal laws, but also **interpreting the Constitution**. By its power of **judicial review**, the Supreme Court can strike down laws passed by Congress — as well as state laws — by declaring them unconstitutional. This is a highly significant power, with political implications. However, just as with the other two branches of government, the Supreme Court does have a number of checks upon it.

The topic is divided into the following four major headings:

A The justices
B The power of judicial review
C Issues concerning civil rights and liberties
D Checks on the Supreme Court

A The justices

1 Membership

There are a number of key points to remember regarding the membership of and the appointment process to the Supreme Court:

- There are **nine members** of the Supreme Court: one chief justice; eight associate justices.
- The number is fixed by Congress and has remained unchanged since 1869.
- They are **appointed by the president**.
- They must be **confirmed by the Senate**.
- They **hold office for life** 'during good behaviour' (Article III, Section 1), meaning they can be impeached, tried and removed from office by Congress; otherwise justices leave the Court only by voluntary retirement or death.

Franklin Roosevelt tried to increase the number, but Congress refused to agree to it.

Justice	Date appointed	President appointing
William Rehnquist	1971 as Associate Justice 1986 as Chief Justice	Nixon (R) Reagan (R)
John Paul Stevens	1975	Ford (R)
Sandra Day O'Connor	1981	Reagan (R)
Antonin Scalia	1986	Reagan (R)
Anthony Kennedy	1987	Reagan (R)
David Souter	1990	Bush (R)
Clarence Thomas	1991	Bush (R)
Ruth Bader Ginsburg	1993	Clinton (D)
Stephen Breyer	1994	Clinton (D)

Table 8.1 Supreme Court membership (2001)

2 *Appointment process*

The appointment process is conducted as follows:

(1) The president must wait for a vacancy to occur: on average about once every 2 years, though Carter (1977–81) made no appointments and no vacancies occurred between 1994 and 2001.

(2) The president's closest aides begin the search for suitable candidates.

(3) A short list is drawn up and candidates are subjected to a detailed interview and FBI background checks.

(4) The president announces the nominee at a public gathering at the White House.

(5) The American Bar Association (ABA) traditionally offered a professional rating of the nominee (see Table 8.2):

- 'well qualified'
- 'qualified'
- 'not qualified'

(6) The nominee (plus other witnesses) appears before a hearing at the Senate Judiciary Committee.

(7) The Senate Judiciary Committee votes on whether or not to recommend confirmation.

(8) The nomination is debated on the floor of the Senate.

(9) A final vote is taken — a **simple majority** is required for confirmation.

George W. Bush has said he will use the Federalist Society to perform this function.

The Senate Judiciary Committee's vote is only a recommendation, though it is rarely over-turned.

Nominee	Year	ABA rating	Senate Judiciary Committee vote	Senate vote
Ginsburg	1993	Well qualified	18–0	96–3
Thomas	1991	Qualified	7–7	52–48
Souter	1990	Well qualified	13–1	90–9
Bork	1987	Well qualified	5–9	42–58

Table 8.2 ABA ratings and Senate votes on selected Supreme Court nominees

When the president is searching for a new member of the Supreme Court, where will he look? There are five possible pools of recruitment:

- The federal Appeals Court (e.g. Clarence Thomas, 1991)
- The state courts (e.g. Sandra Day O'Connor, 1981)
- The executive branch (e.g. William Rehnquist, 1971)
- Academia (e.g. a law professor at a prestigious university)
- Congress (e.g. a member of the Senate Judiciary Committee)

The Senate has rejected 29 Supreme Court nominees since 1789, the most recent being that of Robert Bork in 1987. Before that, President Nixon lost two nominees in as many years — Clement Haynesworth (45–55) in 1969 and Harrold Carswell (45–51) in 1970. In 1987, Douglas Ginsburg withdrew from the nomination after admitting illegal drug use during his confirmation hearing at the Senate Judiciary Committee.

No relation to Ruth Bader Ginsburg.

3 *Philosophy of justices*

These are technical, legal terms. Think of the word 'construction' as meaning 'interpretation'.

It is often suggested that presidents look for justices who share their judicial philosophy. In this respect, justices are classified as to whether they are 'liberals' or 'conservatives'. Another classification used is of **'loose constructionists'** and **'strict constructionists'** (see Table 8.3).

Classification	Ideology	Characteristics	Party	Examples
Strict constructionists	conservative	Strict/literal interpretation of the Constitution; favour states' rights	Tend to be appointed by Republican presidents	Rehnquist Scalia Thomas
Loose constructionists	liberal	Read things into the Constitution; favour federal government power	Tend to be a appointed by Democratic presidents	Ginsburg Breyer

Table 8.3 Classification of Supreme Court justices

There are exceptions. President George Bush did not realise when he appointed David Souter to the Court in 1990 that he was appointing one of its most liberal members. Other justices — like Sandra Day O'Connor and Anthony Kennedy — are much less easy to classify. They tend to be referred to as **'swing' justices**.

B The power of judicial review

1 *Definition and origins*

Don't bother to get into the details of this case — they are not important.

Judicial review is the power of the Supreme Court to declare acts of Congress, or actions of the executive — or acts or actions of state governments — unconstitutional, and thereby null and void. This power is nowhere mentioned in the Constitution. One might say that the Court 'found' the power for itself in the 1803 case of *Marbury v. Madison*. This was the first time that the Supreme Court declared an act of Congress unconstitutional.

2 *Usage*

'Strict constructionists' tend to favour 'judicial restraint'; 'loose constructionists' tend to favour 'judicial activism' — but note the word 'tend'.

Since then, the Supreme Court has used this power on hundreds of occasions — at times sparingly (periods of **'judicial restraint'**), but at other times far more frequently (periods of **'judicial activism'**). By using its power of judicial review, the Court can, in effect, update the meaning of the words of the Constitution, most of which were written over two centuries ago. Hence, they will decide what the phrase in the 8th Amendment (written in 1791) forbidding

'cruel and unusual punishments' means today. Likewise, they will decide whether the 1st Amendment right of 'freedom of speech' applies to the Internet. As a former Chief Justice, Charles Evans Hughes, once remarked: 'We are under a Constitution, but the Constitution is what the judges say it is.'

3 *Political importance*

A common focus for essay questions. Don't forget to deal with the appointment process and the power of judicial review — both are important here.

Using its power of judicial review, the Supreme Court has involved itself in a host of political issues. It is this that helps give the Court its political importance because many of the issues dealt with by the Court are the hot-button political issues of the day, matters over which political parties disagree and elections are fought.

The Supreme Court can also be seen as something of a 'political body' because its members are appointed by a politician (the president) and confirmed by other politicians (senators). Appointments to the Supreme Court also become an issue in many presidential elections. This was certainly the case in the 2000 election.

One can see very clearly — some might say too clearly — the political importance of the Supreme Court in the case of *George W. Bush v. Albert Gore Jr* (2000). Five weeks after the presidential election, on 11 December 2000, the Supreme Court ruled that the manual recount scheme devised by the Florida Supreme Court was unconstitutional because it violated the 'equal protection' clause of the 14th Amendment. In the same decision, the Court also ruled that given the time constraints, 'it is evident that any recount seeking to meet the December 12 [deadline] will be unconstitutional'. The Court was seen by some to be literally handing the election to Governor Bush.

In recent decades, the Supreme Court has, for example, handed down judgements of great political significance in such areas as:
- the rights of racial minorities
- the rights of arrested persons
- capital punishment
- abortion rights
- freedom of religion
- freedom of speech, freedom of the press and freedom of expression
- gun control
- the actions of the executive branch, including the president

C Issues concerning civil rights and liberties

1 *The rights of racial minorities*

When using these cases in an answer, don't get side-tracked by the narrative. What happened to whom is really not important. Concentrate on the analytical importance of the case.

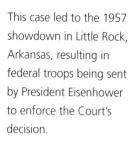

This case led to the 1957 showdown in Little Rock, Arkansas, resulting in federal troops being sent by President Eisenhower to enforce the Court's decision.

- *Brown v. The Board of Education of Topeka* (1954): the Court declared a law of the state of Kansas to be unconstitutional because it transgressed the 'equal protection' clause of the 14th Amendment. It led to the desegregation of schools across the USA, especially in the Deep South. 'Separate educational facilities are inherently unequal', declared the Court, overturning its 1896 ruling of 'separate but equal'.
- *Swann v. Charlotte-Mecklenberg Board of Education* (1971): the Court extended the ban on segregated schools from *de jure* segregation (mainly in the South) to *de facto* segregation (mainly in the cities of the Northeast) caused by the widespread policy of neighbourhood schooling. It led to the introduction of school busing programmes to provide racially mixed schools in all areas.

This case led to widespread anti-busing protests in many US cities in the Northeast, notably Boston, where protesters burnt the buses — thankfully before the children were on board!

- *Adarand Constructors v. Peña* (1995): the Court struck down a federal government affirmative action programme on the employment of minority workers. This case led to President Clinton's remark about affirmative action: 'Mend it, don't end it.'
- *Gratz v. Bollinger* (2003): the Court ruled that the University of Michigan's affirmative action-based undergraduate admissions programme was unconstitutional because it was too 'mechanistic'.

2 The rights of arrested persons

'Miranda rights', as the police now call them, have probably featured in a number of US-made crime films you might have seen.

- *Gideon v. Wainwright* (1963): the Court interpreted the 14th Amendment as guaranteeing the right to legal representation.
- *Miranda v. Arizona* (1966): the Court interpreted the 5th Amendment right to remain silent as extending to the right to be reminded of that right when arrested.

3 Capital punishment

It is important to include the phrase 'as then imposed'. The case did not declare capital punishment *per se* to be unconstitutional.

- *Furman v. Georgia* (1972): the Court decided that the death penalty, as then imposed, was a 'cruel and unusual punishment', and thereby violated the 8th Amendment. The consequences of this case included the more widespread use of lethal injection and of two-stage trials, in which, during a second stage, mitigating circumstances are considered before the sentence is decided.
- *Atkins v. Virginia* (2002): the Court ruled that the execution of mentally retarded criminals was unconstitutional.
- *Roper v. Simmons* (2005): the Court ruled that it was unconstitutional to sentence anyone to death for a crime they committed when younger than 18.

4 Abortion rights

The phrase 'personal choice' gives rise to those who support abortion rights calling themselves 'pro-choice'.

- *Roe v. Wade* (1973): the Court struck down a Texas state law forbidding abortion. It interpreted the 14th Amendment right of 'liberty' to include 'freedom of personal choice in matters of marriage and family life', and that this right 'necessarily includes the right of a woman to decide whether or not to terminate her pregnancy'. Few cases have been of such profound political importance.

'Pro-life' = anti-abortionists.

- **Webster v. Reproductive Health Services (1989):** the Court upheld a state law of Missouri forbidding the involvement of any 'public employee' or 'public facility' in the performance of an abortion 'not necessary to save the life of the mother'. Pro-choice supporters regarded this as the Court nibbling away at *Roe v. Wade*.
- **Planned Parenthood of Southeastern Pennsylvania v. Casey (1992):** the Court upheld a Pennsylvania state law that required a married woman seeking an abortion to notify her husband beforehand, receive counselling on the risks and alternatives and to wait 24 hours after receiving counselling. Women under 18 also had to have parental consent for an abortion. This again was opposed by the pro-choice lobby. But the pro-life supporters were also angry, as they wanted the Court to go all the way and overturn *Roe v. Wade*.

5 Freedom of religion

The term 'public school' in the USA is equivalent to 'state school' in the UK.

'Graduation ceremonies' in US schools are ceremonies for students at the end of their school career.

- **Engel v. Vitale (1962):** the Court, in nullifying a New York state law, declared that government-sponsored prayer in public schools violated the 1st Amendment clause against 'an establishment of religion'.
- **Wallace v. Jaffree (1985):** the Court declared an Alabama state law providing for a period of silent meditation at the start of the school day in public schools to be unconstitutional.
- **Lee v. Weisman (1992):** the Court declared prayer at public school graduation ceremonies unconstitutional.
- **Epperson v. Arkansas (1968):** the Court declared unconstitutional a state law of Arkansas to ban the teaching of Darwinism.
- **Edwards v. Aguillard (1987):** the Court declared a Louisiana state law unconstitutional that required the creation story to be taught alongside theories of evolution.
- **Allegheny County v. American Civil Liberties Union (1989):** the Court declared Allegheny (Pennsylvania) County's Christmas display an infringement of 1st Amendment rights because it contained only religious figures, whereas in 1984 (*Lynch v. Donnelly*) the Court had okayed the City of Pawtucket's (Rhode Island) display, which included religious figures but also Santa Claus and a Christmas tree.
- **Zelman v. Simmons-Harris (2002):** the Court upheld Ohio's so-called 'school voucher' programme.

6 Freedom of speech, freedom of the press and freedom of expression

This case is always quoted by opponents of campaign finance reform.

- **Buckley v. Valeo (1976):** the Court declared unconstitutional that part of the 1974 Federal Election Campaign Act which limited expenditure by candidates in presidential elections, claiming that limits violated 'freedom of speech' rights.
- **Rankin v. McPherson (1987):** the Court upheld the right of Ardith McPherson not to be sacked for making comments about the assassination attempt on

President George Bush described the Court's decision as 'wrong, dead wrong'.

The *Washington Post* headlined the decision as 'The First Amendment Goes Digital'.

President Reagan in 1981, claiming that his 1st Amendment rights of freedom of speech had been infringed.

- ***Texas v. Johnson* (1989):** a Texas state law forbidding the burning of the US flag was declared unconstitutional by the Court.
- ***United States v. Eichman* (1990):** the 1989 Flag Protection Act was declared unconstitutional.
- ***Reno v. American Civil Liberties Union* (1997):** the 1996 Communications Decency Act was declared unconstitutional. The Act made it a crime to make 'indecent' or 'patently offensive' material available to minors on the Internet. But the Court claimed that this infringed the 1st Amendment rights of adults because the law was too vague in its definitions.
- ***Ashcroft v. Free Speech Coalition* (2002):** the Court declared the Child Pornography Protection Act of 1996 unconstitutional.

7 Gun control

- ***United States v. Lopez* (1995):** the Court declared unconstitutional the 1990 Gun-Free School Zones Act, stating that Congress had exceeded its power under Article I, Section 8. This case was one that also had clear implications for the scope of federal government power over state and local jurisdictions.
- ***Printz v. United States* (1997):** the Court declared unconstitutional part of the 1993 Brady Act requiring local law enforcement officers to conduct background checks on would-be hand-gun purchasers during a 5-day waiting period. Here was another ruling clearly affecting the federal–state government balance.

D Checks on the Supreme Court

1 By Congress

- The Senate confirms all Supreme Court appointments.
- The House can impeach justices and the Senate try them and, if found guilty by a two-thirds majority, remove them from office.
- Congress can alter the number of justices on the Court.
- Congress can initiate constitutional amendments, thereby seeking to over-turn judgements of the Court with which it disagrees, such as recent (though unsuccessful) attempts concerning flag desecration, school prayers, abortion rights and congressional term limits.

See Table 1.2.

2 By the president

- Nominates all justices.
- Can decide either to throw his political weight behind the Court (e.g. Eisenhower

over the 1954 *Brown v. Board* decision) or to criticise it openly (e.g. Nixon over 'busing' in 1972, and Bush over flag-burning in 1990).

● Has the power of pardon (see Topic 6.A.10).

3 *Other checks*

● The Court has no enforcement powers (e.g. in the *Brown v. Board* decision it was dependent upon Eisenhower sending in federal troops to desegregate the Little Rock Central High School in 1957).

● The Court has no initiation power. It has to wait for cases to come before it. It cannot rule on hypothetical issues.

● Public opinion can sometimes be seen as a check on the Court (e.g. the *Casey* decision on abortion rights in 1992).

● The Constitution itself — some parts of the document are unambiguous and not open to interpretation.

● The Supreme Court may check itself, as it did in the *Brown v. Board* decision in 1954, overturning its earlier (1896) decision in *Plessy v. Ferguson*.

Your study of American government and politics has followed on from — or may have been in parallel with — a study of the government and politics of the United Kingdom. The danger is that you may not have made as many connections between the two as you might. At various appropriate places in these Revision Notes, comparisons have been drawn upon from the UK. You should seek to do so in your essays.

The A2 examinations include an element of **synoptic assessment**. Synoptic assessment involves the explicit drawing together of knowledge, understanding and skills learned in different parts of your AS and A2 courses in government and politics.

One thing that will help you in this 'drawing together' will be to keep in mind some **key political concepts** that are central to both American government and politics and to the government and politics of the United Kingdom and other western European democracies.

This topic deals with seven key political concepts:

- **A** Accountability
- **B** Authority
- **C** Power
- **D** Democracy
- **E** Representation
- **F** Rights
- **G** Pluralism

A Accountability

Juvenal's famous question *'quis custodiet ipsos custodes?'* — 'who will guard the guardians?' — is about accountability.

Politicians are meant to be 'accountable'. Accountability is best thought of as **being answerable** or, if you prefer, **answerability**. It implies that those in positions of power have a duty to explain their actions and open themselves to potential criticism. But the word 'accountability' raises a number of subsidiary questions. To whom are they accountable? How are they accountable? For what are they accountable? Essentially, they are responsible to 'the people', or more specifically 'the electorate'. This gives a clue to the answer to the second question, for one of the means of accountability is through elections. But it is more than that. In a democratic system of government characterised by the doctrine of the separation of powers, each branch of government may have a role in calling the other branches to account. So in the UK House of Commons, the system of departmental select committees is meant to make the government (prime minister, cabinet) accountable for its decisions and actions. And we have seen numerous opportunities for accountability to take place in American government. These include:

- investigations of the executive branch conducted by congressional standing or select committees

- the House of Representatives' power to impeach any federal executive or judicial official — including the president — and the Senate's power to try them and, if found guilty, remove them from office
- congressional primary elections, in which incumbent members of the House and the Senate have to fight for the right to appear on the ballot in the general election

Accountability is clearly enhanced by 'knowledge' and 'information'. In a country such as the United States, with a Freedom of Information Act, accountability is likely to be more rigorous than in the UK, with its Official Secrets Act.

B Authority

Authority is **the right to exercise power**. Another key political concept closely allied with authority is therefore **legitimacy**. All political office-holders have a certain degree of authority. In a democracy where office-holders will often be elected, the election itself bestows a certain authority or legitimacy on the office-holder. People are often described as being 'in authority', in other words their right to rule can be traced back to the particular office — prime minister, president, senator.

A further matter regarding the concept of authority which is often discussed is 'where does it come from?' Those on the left in politics — people we would describe as liberals or social democrats — tend to believe that authority 'rises from below', from 'the people'. Those on the right in politics — people we would describe as conservatives — tend to believe that authority 'comes from above' by virtue of political wisdom, social experience or position. (Indeed, if this line of thought were taken one stage further, we would arrive at a belief in 'divine right' — authority bestowed by God.)

It is very important to distinguish 'authority' from 'power'.

C Power

In answering an essay question including the word 'power', 'powerful' or 'powers', it is always a good idea to spend a few sentences at least making these distinctions clear. Examiners will reward this.

Whereas **authority is the *right* to exercise power, power is the *ability* to exercise power**. But not only must we distinguish 'power' from 'authority', it is very useful in the study of politics to be clear about the distinction between 'power' and 'powers'. **Powers are the functions, tasks or jobs of an office. Power**, on the other hand, **is the ability to get things done**. Every American president has the same powers as his predecessor. Essentially, President George W. Bush has the same *powers* as Jimmy Carter had, as Harry Truman had, as Woodrow Wilson had, as Abraham Lincoln had, as George Washington had — the powers to sign and veto bills, to appoint cabinet officers and Supreme Court justices, to negotiate treaties and so on. But the *power* that each president possesses is very much a variable. Indeed, it even varies for the same president throughout his period of office. One might argue, for example, that Nixon (after Watergate), or Reagan (after Iran-Contra), or Clinton (after Lewinsky), had much less power than before those unfortunate episodes.

Power is the ability to get people to do the things they wouldn't otherwise do. In his scholarly book on the American presidency (*Presidential Power*), Professor Richard Neustadt makes it clear that 'powers are no guarantee of power'. In other words, the jobs one has to do as president are no guarantee of actually getting things done. We saw this in Topic 6.E.1. That is why the president has to resort to **persuasion**. As Neustadt again claims: 'The president's power is the power to persuade.' He does allow that 'powers may lead to power', but they are no guarantee of it.

Checks and balances are all about the **limitation of power**. In this sense, one could make out a good case for the British prime minister being potentially more powerful in terms of pursuing their domestic policy agenda than is the American president.

D Democracy

Democracy is, in its simplest definition, **rule by the people**. But that poses other questions: 'What does it mean to rule?' and 'Which people?' President Lincoln's famous remark about 'government of the people, by the people and for the people' is often quoted as an elaboration on our basic definition. The theory of democracy enshrines another important principle — that of **popular participation** in free, fair and frequent elections in which there is political equality for all ('one person, one vote') and freedom of choice between candidates.

So we can begin to judge how 'democratic' a country is by using these criteria. In the United States, we have seen that a large number of national public officials are subject to direct election — the president and vice-president (though still in theory through the Electoral College), senators (since 1914), members of the House. This contrasts quite sharply with the situation in the UK, where no members of the executive branch are directly elected to their executive posts and only members of one of the two legislative chambers — the House of Commons — are directly elected. Indeed, it is worth noting that in the United States the second chamber was reformed almost a century ago to be **directly elected**. Recent reform of the UK's second chamber, however, has been to move from a mix of hereditary and appointed members to a chamber made up only of **appointed** members.

Like cars, democracy comes in many different models. You do not need to know about all of them at this stage, but it is important that you know about two in particular. In **direct democracy** (sometimes referred to as **participatory democracy**), the people participate directly in making decisions. This was seen in its purest form in the town meeting in ancient Athens. Today it is seen in the use of **referendums** in the UK and in **initiatives** used in the individual states of America, though not at the federal level.

The quotation comes from Lincoln's Gettysburg address in 1864.

Although the prime minister and most cabinet ministers have been directly elected as MPs.

The most famous initiative in recent American political history was Proposition 13, approved by the voters of California in 1978 to limit the state's property taxes.

A more common model of democracy nowadays is **representative democracy**. This is best thought of as a form of **indirect democracy**. In this model, the people choose their representatives to make decisions on their behalf. This is the form that exists today in the USA, the UK and several other western European democracies.

Andrew Heywood (*Key Concepts in Politics*, Macmillan, 2000) claims the advantages of democracy are that:
- it defends freedom by constraining power
- it promotes popular participation and citizenship
- it strengthens a sense of community
- it guarantees a high level of political stability

Among the disadvantages, Heywood suggests that:
- it gives power to the 'ignorant and poorly informed masses'
- it amounts to 'tyranny of the 51%' — or even less in some cases
- it easily leads to excessive bureaucracy, too much 'compromise' and sometimes 'gridlock'

> See also the section on 'Representation' below.

> No political party in a UK general election has won more than 50% of the popular vote since 1945. The last three presidential elections in the USA have all resulted in the election of a president with less than 50% of the popular vote — in George W. Bush's case, fewer votes than his opponent!

E Representation

This is another very important key concept upon which we have already touched in Section D. But again we need to clarify its meaning quite carefully. What does it mean to call a politician — whether in Parliament or Congress — a 'representative' of the people? What does it mean to say that one of their functions is to 'represent' their constituents?

The word 'representative' is thought to have four distinct meanings.

(1) A representative may act as a **trustee**, using their own mature judgement rather than following the 'popular whim'.

(2) A representative may act as a **delegate**, acting purely on the instructions of others. Hence the term 'delegate' being used by those who attend the American National Party Conventions, having been instructed for whom they should vote (see Topic 2.A.3).

(3) A representative may act upon the basis of a **mandate**. This mandate will have been gained not by the representative themselves, but by the political party under whose banner they stood at the last election. This model of representation is based on the belief that a party, in winning an election, gains a mandate to carry out the policies which it presented at the election.

(4) There is what is called the **resemblance** model of representation. This model would suggest that a legislative chamber should be a **cross-section** or **microcosm** of the nation as a whole. This might be reflected in its make-up, for example in terms of gender, race and geographic region. The extent to which Congress — or the UK Parliament or its regional assemblies — is 'representative' in this sense is a matter of constant debate. It throws up such questions as:
- Does it matter that in 2001, only 59 of the 435 members of the House of Representatives were women?

- And what about the fact that at the same time there were no African-American members of the Senate, a group that makes up around 10% of the national population?
- Can only women represent women? Can only Hispanics represent Hispanics?
- Should 'affirmative action' programmes now be instituted to redress such 'unrepresentativeness'?

The UK Labour Party experimented with 'women-only short lists' in the 1990s.

F Rights

Inalienable = non-transferable, undeniable.

A right is **something to which one is entitled**. The term 'human rights' is therefore used to refer to the entitlements of all humans as humans. (The same could be said, I suppose, of animals and animal rights.) Human rights are often therefore described as being **fundamental** and **inalienable**.

As the American Declaration of Independence has it: 'We hold these truths to be self-evident, that all men are created equal, that they are endowed by their Creator with **certain unalienable rights**, that among these are life, liberty and the pursuit of happiness.'

The term 'rights' is also closely linked with **freedoms**. In the **Bill of Rights**, the Founding Fathers wanted to protect, guarantee and entrench certain fundamental rights and freedoms such as:

- freedom of religion, speech, the press and assembly (1st Amendment)
- the 'right to keep and bear arms' (2nd Amendment)
- the right to remain silent (5th Amendment)
- the right of a 'speedy and public trial' (6th Amendment)

A distinction can be made between negative and positive rights. **Negative rights mark out 'freedoms from'** and **limit** the role of government, for example freedom from 'cruel and unusual punishments' (8th Amendment). **Positive rights mark out 'freedoms to'** and **make demands on** the role of government, for example the right to education.

See Topic 8.C.

How and by whom are rights protected? In the United States, we can see that all three branches of government have a role to play: Congress by the passage of appropriate legislation; the executive by proper enforcement of the laws; the courts by interpreting both the laws and the Constitution. Clearly, in a country with a written Constitution embodying a Bill of Rights, the courts have a very important role to play in the protection of rights and freedoms.

G Pluralism

Pluralism is best thought of as **diversity**. Its opposite is **élitism**, best thought of as 'a few'. To describe a country as being pluralist is therefore to suggest that the political resources within that country — money, expertise, access to the mass

media etc. — are widely spread, and are in the hands of many diverse individuals and groups. This prevents there being a **governing élite**, which would have a **monopoly** of political power.

Pluralism is also associated with **decentralisation**. In the United States, there are so many levels of government that no single group can ever dominate. In a pluralist society, therefore, there is a great need for negotiation, compromising, deals and persuasion.

Pluralism, however, does not necessarily suggest that all these competing groups are equal. They quite clearly are not. Indeed, some see the system as merely one of **competing élites** — political parties, pressure groups, bureaucrats, business people, the media, trade unionists, educators, lawyers and so on. Harking back to what we studied earlier, one could then ask to what extent these 'competing élites' are 'representative' of their own client groups.

The problem with pluralism is that it can easily lead to what many see as the **atomisation** of both politics and society. And this in turn leads to gridlock — the failure of government to be able to do anything at all. Pluralist democracy may be 'nice', but it sure can be frustrating! But then, as Winston Churchill once remarked: 'No one pretends that democracy is perfect or all-wise. Indeed, it has been said that democracy is the worst form of government except for all those other forms that have been tried from time to time.'

A sound point on which to end.

In a speech in the House of Commons, 11 November 1947.